THE WACKIEST GAMES!
THE CRAZIEST CALLS!
THE WILDEST RIVALRIES!

THE FOOTBALL HALL OF SHAME™ 2

Q. What Hall of Famer became the first and only man in NFL history to get injured during a coin-tossing ceremony? (see chapter on *Flip Flops*)

Q. What rowdy football game triggered a pistol duel between two high-ranking military men? (see chapter on *Campus Capers*)

Q. What college football player was so upset over a loss that he sawed a 1953 Chevy in half? (see chapter on *Wild Cards*)

Q. What NFL quarterback was stuffed into a locker after mouthing off to Coach Lou Saban at halftime? (see chapter on *Headless Coaches*)

Q. What play-by-play announcer accidentally set his pants on fire during a *Monday Night Football* broadcast? (see chapter on *Media Madness*)

Books by Bruce Nash and Allan Zullo

The Baseball Hall of Shame™
The Baseball Hall of Shame™ 2
The Baseball Hall of Shame™ 3
The Baseball Hall of Shame™ 4
The Football Hall of Shame™
The Football Hall of Shame™ 2
The Golf Hall of Shame™
The Sports Hall of Shame™
Baseball Confidential™
The Misfortune 500™

Published by POCKET BOOKS

THE
FOOTBALL
HALL OF SHAME™ 2

by
BRUCE NASH AND ALLAN ZULLO
BERNIE WARD, CURATOR

POCKET BOOKS

New York   London   Toronto   Sydney   Tokyo   Singapore

An *Original* Publication of POCKET BOOKS

POCKET BOOKS, a division of Simon & Schuster Inc.
1230 Avenue of the Americas, New York, NY 10020

ISBN: 0-671-69413-8

First Pocket Books trade paperback printing September 1990

10 9 8 7 6 5 4 3 2 1

The Football Hall of Shame is a trademark of
Nash and Zullo Productions, Inc.

POCKET and colophon are registered trademarks of
Simon & Schuster Inc.

Printed in the U.S.A.

To Greg Nash, an All-Star jeweler, an All-Pro songwriter, and—most of all—a Hall of Fame brother.

—B.N.

To my brother Mike Zullo, who has tackled some mighty big demons and thrown them for a loss.

—A.Z.

ACKNOWLEDGMENTS

We wish to thank all the fans, players, coaches, and sportswriters who contributed nominations.

We are especially grateful to those players, past and present, who shared a few laughs with us as they recounted the inglorious moments that earned them a place in *The Football Hall of SHAME*.

This book couldn't have been completed without the assistance and cooperation of the Pro Football Hall of Fame in Canton, Ohio. We appreciate the help, guidance, and friendship of Joe Horrigan, director of research information; Peter Fierle, library research assistant; and Sandi Self, librarian. For their cooperation, we thank Doug Lang, of the NFL Alumni Association, and Dick Cohen, president of the Sports Bookshelf in Ridgefield, Connecticut, who allowed us access to his wonderful collection of football books.

Special thanks go to: Bud Asher, Lea Booth, Colin Cameron, Jack Clary, John Clayton, John Crumpacker, Jeff Doubek, Jim Ford, Karmen Fowler, Reid Handley, Tommy Hood, Bob James, Bob McCoy, Dev Nelson, Floyd Sageser, Ernie Salvatore, Glenn Stone, Maurice Toler, and Lou Vales.

And for running interference for us, we thank our teammates in life, Sophie Nash and Kathy Zullo.

CONTENTS

KICKING OFF

. . . And the shame continues.

Since *The Football Hall of SHAME* was published in 1986, we knew it would be only a matter of time before we compiled a second volume of outrageous, rip-roaring gridiron gaffes.

Fortunately for all of us fans who love to laugh, college and pro football provide a never-ending supply of embarrassingly funny moments. They happen to coaches, rookies, and veterans. Even Super Bowl quarterbacks. John Elway of the Denver Broncos and Phil Simms of the New York Giants both suffered a quarterback's silliest faux pas—each mistakenly lined up over a guard to take the snap.

We've received hundreds of nominations from readers and from fans whom we met on our cross-country travels to football stadiums. From the locker rooms and practice fields, players and coaches have tipped us off to other great stories of unforgettable blunders. Many more wacky incidents surfaced when we spent days digging through the archives at the Pro Football Hall of Fame in Canton, Ohio.

Just what does it mean to be in The Football Hall of SHAME? It's a special recognition of a moment we can all identify with—and laugh about—because each of us has at one time or another screwed up.

Hall of Famers are no exception. For example, Len Dawson, the Kansas City Chiefs' great quarterback, holds the NFL record for most fumbles in a game—a magnificent seven. When we interviewed him about this ignominious moment, Dawson gave a hearty laugh and said, "I'm in the record book, so I might as well be in your book, too." And Hall of Famer Doug Atkins, who at training camp fired his gun at night to silence rookies and their loud rock music, said he was "honored" to make it into The Football Hall of SHAME, "even though I had to shoot my way in."

Interestingly, some of the Hall of Shamers could easily make it into The Television Hall of Fame. Inductees who left the gridiron to make their mark on TV include Fred Dryer *(Hunter),* Alex Karras *(Webster),* and Frank Gifford and Dan Dierdorf *(Monday Night Football).* And let's not forget Elizabeth Taylor. That's right. The dazzling star of movies and television has been inducted into The Football Hall of SHAME for wreaking havoc during a coin toss. Karras, by the way, has carved two niches in the Hall—one for tricking a teammate into going AWOL and another for beating up a Chicago Bear only to discover it was his own brother.

Many former players who had long been forgotten were delighted to hear they had been selected for induction. At least, they reasoned, they would be remembered for something even if it was just an inglorious but nutty moment.

For instance, we tracked down All-America running back Bob Fenimore, of Oklahoma A & M. During a 1944 game, Fenimore was heading for a sure touchdown when he dove over what he thought was the goal line—but it was only the 10-yard line. "My God," he told us, "I thought everyone would have forgotten that by now." Denver Broncos offensive guard Tom Glassic, who in 1976 was late for Super Bowl XII because he overslept, said he was glad to receive Hall of SHAME dishonors. "At least that embarrassing moment has finally paid off after all these years," he said. Then there was Jim Hogan, punter for the University of Central Florida, who had a good sense of history and humor. He was inducted for bowing to the crowd before attempting to boot his final collegiate punt in 1986. But the kick was blocked and returned for a touchdown. After his interview with us, Hogan said, "If I had known I would make it into The Football Hall of SHAME, I would've done something more dramatic. I would've kicked that ball to my friends in the stands."

America's favorite spectator sport will continue to produce more hilarious happenings on and off the field. And we will continue to chronicle these zany moments of both the superstars and the bozos. As our motto says: "Fame *and* shame are part of the game."

PRANKS FOR THE MEMORIES

They are the jokers of football. They love to pull off pranks as much as they do last-second victories. They throw more bull than pigskin. And they catch more flak than touchdown passes. No superstar, no rookie, no roommate is safe from being victimized by these audacious pranksters. For "The Most Madcap Jokesters," The Football Hall of SHAME inducts the following:

JOE MONTANA

Quarterback ■ San Francisco 49ers ■ 1979–present

Opposing players aren't the only ones who have been burned by the clever plays of Joe Montana. His fellow 49ers have been victimized, too—by his pranks.

Joe has this thing about teammates' bicycles. He steals them. He hides them. He leaves them high in the trees.

Most of his shenanigans have taken place on the campus of Sierra College in Rocklin, California, where the 49ers train in the preseason. The players stay in dormitories on the campus of the junior college, which is about a third of a mile to the practice field.

Because it's too far to walk on hot days after practice, the players rent sturdy mountain bikes from a local bicycle company. For some unfathomable reason, Montana can't resist doing nasty things to these spiffy red bicycles. Like hiding them. As a result, his victimized teammates have had to trudge a third of a mile in the stifling hot weather and end up sweaty before practice even begins.

"It's become a tradition with him," said wide receiver Mike Wilson, who claims to have witnessed most of Joe's bike capers since joining the team in 1981.

During the 1989 training camp, Wilson said, Joe let the air out of the tires of everyone's bicycles. But that's not all Montana did. "Every other day, you'd find your bike up in a tree," complained linebacker Jim Fahnhorst. "It was so damn dark when you came out of our [evening] meetings that it took you 15 to 20 minutes to find a bike and then, when you did find it, you discovered that it wasn't yours."

The celebrated quarterback has been hiding bikes in trees—and even on roofs of campus buildings—for years, said Wilson. Montana often waits until the last week of training camp to stash the bikes in trees because that's when the players are the most tired.

"On the last day of training camp, there must have been ten bikes up in the trees," said Wilson. "Joe had some help from [backup quarterback] Steve Young."

The year before, added safety Tom Holmoe, Montana tried something new. "Joe came out with a 30-foot-long chain and locked all the bikes together. He got a laugh out of that."

Because quarterbacks are the first players to get out of meetings, Montana has always had the best opportunity to snatch bikes. "Joe doesn't have a bike in Rocklin, so he'll ride everyone else's," said linebacker Michael Walter. "But then the bikes end up in trees and everyone blames Joe."

When a reporter for *The Football Hall of SHAME 2* confronted Montana with the accusations of his teammates, Joe coolly replied, "I plead the fifth. I know that somebody once got a big chain and locked all the bikes together. But," he added with a wink and his tongue firmly planted in his cheek, "I'm not sure who did that one."

With the same precision that he has used to pick apart opposing teams' defenses, Montana victimized the 49ers defense during practice late in the 1989 season. "Joe put all the bikes of the defensive players in the trees while they were in a meeting," said safety Ronnie Lott. "That was pretty funny."

One year, when Montana decided to cool it on the bike antics, he took up water pistols. Recalled Fahnhorst, "I remember Joe and [linebacker] Riki Ellison went wild with squirt guns. Joe's was like a damn Uzi machine gun. It had a battery pack in it and he could continually hose you down."

Perhaps because Montana is such a superstar, his teammates have been slow to pay him back. One of the few pranks pulled on Joe in 1989 came at the hands of nose tackle Jim Burt. While Montana was conducting a postgame press conference in the locker room, Burt sneaked up behind Joe and doused him with ice water.

LYLE BLACKWOOD

Defensive Back ■ Cincinnati Bengals–Seattle Seahawks–Baltimore Colts–Miami Dolphins ■ 1973–86

It's a wonder that Lyle Blackwood survived 14 years in the NFL without getting seriously hurt. Not by his opponents—but by his own teammates!

Blackwood pulled some of the league's nastiest and funniest pranks on his fellow players. None was more devilish than the "Wronged

Husband" gag that he played on rookies while he was with the Cincinnati Bengals.

Blackwood lost track of how many teammates fell victim to the practical joke. "But a lot of the guys are household names now," he said. "I swore I'd never reveal who they are. If I told, they'd surely kill me."

Blackwood and his fellow connivers set the scheme in motion by telling a gullible rookie to check out some beautiful woman sitting in the stands. They convinced their pigeon that although the lady was married, she lusted after his body. She wanted Blackwood to set up a date with the rookie as soon as her husband left town.

"I'd go on and on about how this gorgeous gal was really hot for the guy," recalled Blackwood. "Since we usually pulled the gag during preseason training camp, most of the victims had been away from women for weeks and were raring to go."

The buildup continued for days. At last, an excited Blackwood whispered to the heavy-breathing rookie that tonight was the night! Blackwood arranged to escort him to the tryst.

"We used a house on the outskirts of town where one of our guys would hide with a shotgun filled with blanks," Blackwood said. "I'd pick up the rookie and drive him out. He'd be decked out in his finest clothes.

"It was dark when we got there and as we walked up to the door, the guy with the shotgun would come busting out of the house, cussing and screaming that he knew we were there to see his wife.

"He'd fire the gun with the blanks and I'd fall down, crying that I'd been shot. Each time, the poor rookie panicked! He'd take off like a bat out of hell and sometimes we'd have trouble finding him. One guy dove in a briar patch and lay there for an hour, crying and shaking and trying to hide by digging a hole with his bare hands. Another one belly-crawled all the way across a plowed field in his brand-new suit because there wasn't any cover to hide behind.

"The worst one was the rookie who hurdled a barbed wire fence and disappeared through the woods. We found him five hours later still running down a dirt road miles from the house. He was dazed and dirty and his brand-new clothes were all ripped to shreds from tearing through the bushes."

When Blackwood was traded, his puckish sense of humor went with him. In 1980, as a Baltimore Colt, he bamboozled offensive tackle George Kunz with a disgusting doughnut trick.

"I saw a couple of day-old doughnuts sitting around," recalled Blackwood. "The longer I looked at them the more certain I was that there had to be a good joke there."

The Colts had a vat of hot paraffin in which players stuck a hand or foot if they had a sprain or torn ligaments. The wax sealed in the warmth and hastened the healing process.

"You can imagine all the nasty crap floating around in the wax with guys sticking their feet and other body parts in it," Blackwood said. "It wasn't very appetizing. But I dipped the doughnuts in it and they came out with a layer of wax that looked just like icing."

Blackwood arranged the doughnuts on a plate next to the coffee urn and left for a meeting. When he returned, he learned that Kunz had eaten the waxy doughnuts.

"The amazing thing was he never realized he was eating that awful wax," Blackwood laughed. "He just gulped both of those doughnuts down without tasting them. When I told him what he'd eaten and where the wax came from, George gagged and chased me out of the clubhouse."

During a stint with the Miami Dolphins, Blackwood pulled one of the oldest locker-room pranks in the book, which aroused Coach Don Shula's ire and sent defensive back Robert Sowell dashing for an ice bag to cool his scorched crotch.

"It was the old atomic-balm-in-the-jockstrap trick," said Blackwood. "And if Robert hadn't been late for practice, he'd probably never have fallen for it. But he came running into the locker room with only a minute to get suited up and make it to a team meeting. He pulled on his jockstrap without checking it first. The instant the balm hit him, he knew what had happened. We were all in the next room, but we heard him go, 'ooooooowwwwooooeeeeee!'"

Sowell grabbed a towel and tried to rub off the deep-heating balm. But that only worked the ointment in deeper on his most sensitive parts. His next mistake was to leap in a cold shower. That only heightened the burning sensation.

When the meeting broke up, Blackwood found Sowell spread-eagled across the trainer's table with a pair of ice bags between his legs and globs of Vaseline covering all the exposed parts.

"Of course, Robert couldn't make it out to practice and when Shula caught wind of it, the coach really chewed me out," said Blackwood.

"Later, a bunch of us were standing along the sideline when Robert came out wearing a pair of shorts. I apologized and asked him how he was feeling. He said, 'OK, but I wish they hadn't made me wear this thing.'

"He yanked down the front of his drawers and out popped this big hand that bobbed up and down like it wanted to shake hands with you. The trainer had filled a surgical glove with a cooling lotion and taped it onto Robert's most prominent part.

"Naturally, we started howling, and everybody else ran over to see what was so funny. That hand sticking out from Robert's crotch pretty much broke up practice, which really pissed off Shula. He threatened to run me out of Miami."

From then on, every Dolphin diligently checked his jockstrap before putting it on. Especially Robert Sowell.

WATERFLOGGED

Dousing an unsuspecting teammate with a bucket of cold water was a favorite prank of the Baltimore Colts in 1955.

However, coach Weeb Ewbank announced that the water-throwing was getting out of hand and threatened to levy a $1000 fine on the next guy who was caught in the act.

Despite the warning, linebacker Gino Marchetti convinced teammate Carl Taseff to pull off the joke one more time. The plan called for Taseff to hide behind a corner of the locker room with a full bucket. When rookie Alan Ameche walked in, Marchetti would give a signal and Taseff would drench him.

But the joke was on Taseff. Marchetti waited until Ewbank—all dressed up in a sports coat—stepped into the locker room. Marchetti signaled to Taseff, who leaped from behind the corner and let fly with the water a split second before he realized it was Ewbank.

In a panic, Taseff rushed after the flying water with the bucket, which, of course, was a futile effort. So he dropped to his knees and cried, "I'm so sorry, Coach! I'm so sorry!"

Sputtering and wet, Ewbank thundered, "You're sorry, all right. You're a sorry, dirty, no-good SOB!"

But after he dried off and cooled off, Ewbank forgot all about the fine.

HOUSTON OILERS OFFENSIVE LINE

October 1989

Houston Oiler Greg Montgomery wound up looking more like an Egyptian mummy than a punter after his teammates got through with him. They turned him into a gridiron King Tut as a payback for the heinous crime of misappropriating their lunch money.

Once each week during practice, Montgomery and fellow kicker Tony Zendejas collected $3 from each offensive lineman and made a lunch run to a nearby McDonald's.

One day, tackle Dean Steinkuhler bought his own lunch and discovered that the same meal cost only $2.35. Had Montgomery and Zendejas been pocketing the other 65 cents per player?

"We didn't miss the money. It was the principle of the thing," complained Steinkuhler. "They ripped us off and somebody had to pay for it."

Montgomery was the obvious target since he organized the lunch runs and collected the meal money.

Before practice the following day, the players grabbed Montgomery as he stepped into the locker room. While a quartet of huge linemen held him down, others wrapped rolls of tape around Montgomery until he looked like a poor imitation of The Mummy. Chortling over their fancy gift wrapping, the Oilers ran out to the field to warm up and left their wrapped-up teammate behind.

Eventually, Montgomery freed himself and went around the room cutting every helmet chin strap and shoelace in sight. Howls of outrage echoed through the camp when the victims returned and had to spend precious time fixing straps and replacing shoelaces.

Montgomery had to pay for his misdeeds, growled the linemen. So they hit him where it hurt most—right in the old good luck charm, Bugs Bunny, the punter's favorite stuffed toy.

Montgomery kept Bugs in his locker and each week pinned an obscene slogan on the bunny that insulted the Oilers' upcoming opponent. It was a way of psyching the team up for the game. But the day after the mummy episode, the poor bunny was cut open with a pair of scissors that were left sticking out of his back.

Montgomery taped Bugs back together, replaced the obscene message with one directed at his Houston teammates, and set the bunny back on the shelf of his locker for everyone to see.

Two days later, Bugs was spirited out of the locker room and hung in a kicking net near one end of the practice field. Tackles Bruce "Jumbo" Davis and Doug Smith then brought out a shotgun and took turns blasting away at the dangling bunny until they blew his head off.

The remains were left hanging in the net for a week while Montgomery planned to wear a black armband and play "Taps" at the next game. But after the Oilers lost a critical game to the Cleveland Browns, the punter took down the net, retrieved what was left of his good luck charm, and put Bugs back together again.

"I don't care if he is full of buckshot," Montgomery said. "I need him around for good luck."

DAN DIERDORF

Offensive Tackle–Guard ■ St. Louis Cardinals ■ 1975

No one doubted Dan Dierdorf's sense of humor. But they seriously questioned his sanity when he chopped up Conrad Dobler's best pair of pants minutes before "the meanest man in football" was to appear on national television.

At the time, Dobler was universally hated by all his opponents for biting, gouging, kicking, and clawing during games. Gorgeous Phyllis George and a CBS television crew had come to the St. Louis Cardinals' training camp near St. Charles, Missouri, in 1975 to interview Dobler about his reputation for being the dirtiest player in the league.

The NFL's number-one villain spent hours primping for his big moment before the cameras. Finally, Dierdorf couldn't take any more of the preening Cardinal. So the fun-loving Dan (shown in photo in a wacky disguise) recruited teammate Jackie Smith and the pair watched for the right moment to spring their prank on Dobler.

"Conrad was something of a mental deficient who had no business playing in the NFL—unless he was on your side," joked Dierdorf. "He was lording it over the rest of us about Phyllis George coming all the way to St. Louis just to see him. He was really being an insufferable jerk!

"Dobler spent at least an hour getting every hair in place. But the last straw was when he went into the bathroom and started applying Pearl Drops Tooth Polish. Jackie and I couldn't take any more."

Dobler had planned to wear a carefully selected brand-new pair of $60 jeans to impress George. While Smith stood lookout, Dierdorf attacked the pants with a pair of scissors, cut off the left leg, and then neatly replaced the pants on the hanger so the damage didn't show. Moments later, Dobler pranced back into the locker room and started to dress.

"As luck would have it, Dobler put on the good leg first," recalled Dierdorf. "Then he slid on the snipped leg and when he saw what had happened, he totally lost control. And when Dobler lost control, it was awesome to behold!"

Dobler's instant transformation made the Incredible Hulk look like a wimp. With Dobler's first bellow of rage, the rookies panicked and rushed for the door, with the veterans close behind. Within seconds, the locker room was almost empty and soon a crowd of nude or nearly nude players was milling about on the lawn outside.

Meanwhile, Dobler wreaked havoc inside. He charged a whole row of lockers and tried to knock them over. He picked up benches and hurled them 20 feet across the room. The Cardinals' equipment manager barricaded himself in his room and remained cowering behind locked doors until the rampage ended.

The only player who didn't flee for his life was center Tom Banks. He calmly watched the destruction and shook his head. "I told them not to do it," said Banks. "I warned them this would happen."

Dobler later admitted that he lost control. "Those were brand new jeans! And I didn't have anything else to wear to the interview. When I stuck my foot into the leg Dierdorf had cut off, I really lost it. The way Dierdorf tells it, the rookies, who were scared to death of me anyway, were the first to vacate the room. That's true. But he always fails to mention that he beat most of them out the door.

"Dierdorf was just jealous. Phyllis George wanted to interview a good-looking, articulate, studly gentleman like me, instead of a fat, dumb, ugly flatnose like Dierdorf!"

Overcome by guilt, Jackie Smith offered an extra pair of his pants to the furious Dobler so he could still make the interview. But the trousers were too short and too tight and Dobler could barely sit down.

"I had to keep my legs stuck out in front of me all through the interview because I couldn't bend them at the knees," recalled Dobler. "Phyllis George wondered what I was doing in those skinny Michael Jackson pants."

Dobler kept his Dierdorf-designed jeans for years. When Dierdorf finally hung up his cleats in 1983, Dobler was invited back to St. Louis to participate in the ceremony. At Dierdorf's retirement dinner, Dobler presented him with a beautifully wrapped gift—the altered jeans.

HARD TO SWALLOW

Sportscaster Pat Summerall was at a loss for words during the postgame interview in the Green Bay Packers' locker room after their 35–10 victory in Super Bowl I.

"I was waiting to come on the air with Jimmy Taylor and Elijah Pitts," Summerall recalled. "The sweat was rolling off me as if I'd been playing because the TV lights were so hot.

"Taylor was holding a can of Coca-Cola and said to me, 'Looks like you could use some of this.' I took a big slug of Coke—only it wasn't Coke. He had filled the can with straight bourbon. About ten seconds before I went on the air, my eyes were watering and I couldn't talk."

"I told him, 'I knew it was you all along, you SOB,'" recalled Dobler. "Dierdorf was the only one mean enough—or stupid enough—to do something like that to me."

ALEX KARRAS   EARL MORRALL

Defensive Tackle   **Quarterback**

Detroit Lions ■ Dec. 5, 1965

Detroit Lions stars Alex Karras and Earl Morrall engineered an elaborate hoax that had teammate Sam Williams so convinced he was over the hill that he caught the next plane home and almost took an early retirement.

Williams, a defensive end, was noted for his pass-rushing abilities, his hot temper, and his gullibility. "Sam was so gullible I could sell him the Brooklyn Bridge," said Karras.

In 1965, the Lions picked up Bill Quinlan, another defensive end, whom Williams immediately perceived as a threat to his job. "Why do we need him around?" Williams complained.

As Williams continued to fret over the newcomer, the seeds for a gag began to sprout. On a road trip to the West Coast, Karras and Morrall began to needle the veteran about his possible replacement.

"Maybe they brought Quinlan in to take over your position," Karras suggested to Williams. "Maybe they're working out a trade and you won't be going home with us." Added Morrall, "Maybe they're trying to ease you out. You never know in this business."

The more they talked, the more Williams stewed over what he began to imagine was management's plot to get rid of him. Karras and Morrall stepped up the pressure during a game against the 49ers in San Francisco.

Near the end of the first half, Quinlan was sent in as a substitute for Williams, who went to the sideline in a rage over being replaced. He failed to notice that with a big Detroit lead, most of the other regulars also were being given a breather.

As Williams sat fuming on the bench, Karras sidled alongside him and pointed out that while Quinlan wasn't as good a pass rusher as Williams, he was doing an outstanding job against the run. "He looks really good out there, Sam," Karras observed.

By the fourth quarter, Karras and Morrall had Williams nearly convinced that he was in his last game as a Detroit Lion. And when Quinlan came in as a substitute in the final minutes of the game, Williams was ready to believe anything his conspiring teammates told him. He stomped off the field and hurled his helmet at the bench. "That's the last straw!" Williams roared. "After all I've done for this team!"

After the game, the three went to dinner. Karras and Morrall plied Williams with martinis and more propaganda. It definitely looked like a trade was in the works, said the pranksters.

Somewhere around the seventeenth martini, according to Karras, Williams sobbed, "What would you do, Alex?"

"Well, if it was me," replied Karras with a straight face, "I wouldn't wait for it to happen. I'd get on a plane and go home right now and make them pay for what they're doing."

To a befuddled Williams, the advice made sense. "Take me to the airport," he demanded.

The next day, Williams woke up in his own home in Detroit, wondering how he got there and why. Meanwhile, back in San Francisco, Karras and Morrall chortled over their outlandish practical joke.

Recalled Williams, "The next day, George Wilson [the Lions coach] called and asked me what the hell I was doing in Detroit. I told him I knew what was going on and to just go ahead and trade me.

"Wilson exploded. 'We're not going to trade you,' he yelled. 'But if you don't get your butt back here, we're going to suspend you.'"

So Williams grabbed the next flight back to the coast. But his unexcused absence cost him a $150 fine, plus his round-trip air fare.

Even with all the confusion they had created, Karras and Morrall still weren't finished with the gag. When Williams arrived back at the team's motel, a flashing neon sign on the marquee greeted him with the message, "Welcome Back, Sam."

MINNESOTA VIKINGS OFFENSIVE LINE

Oct. 23, 1989

Rich Karlis, who usually kicks balls *over* the crossbar, found himself in an awkward position—taped from head to toe and dangling upside down from *under* the crossbar like the prize catch in a fishing tournament.

His crime wasn't missing a crucial field goal in an important game. Instead, the Minnesota Vikings kicker was being punished for something his wife said.

For Karlis, it was a valuable lesson in football etiquette. Don't say bad things about those 300-pound offensive linemen who protect your body. Worse yet, don't let your wife call them a bunch of slobs even if they do behave like a bunch of slobs.

Rich's wife, Dena, made the mistake of blabbing to players' wives at a baby shower about her distaste for the offensive linemen and how they were a bad influence on her husband. Since he started hanging out with the gorillas, she said, Rich had let his personal grooming slide and wasn't dressing as fashionably as before.

"She said we were slobs," tackle Gary Zimmerman complained.

When Karlis showed up for practice a few days after the baby shower, the offensive linemen were waiting. Among them was his own brother-in-law, Kirk Lowdermilk, the 6-foot, 3-inch, 270-pound Vikings center and instigator of the "Get Karlis" plot.

The huge linemen seized the 180-pound kicker, taped his hands and feet, blindfolded him, and stuck a gag in his mouth. Then the pigskin posse tossed a rope over the crossbar of a goalpost, strung up the varmint by his feet, and pinned a sign to his jersey that said, "Wife talked about offensive line."

Karlis dangled in the breeze while someone fetched the team photographer. The linemen proudly posed for pictures with their catch before finally releasing him.

"We figured he was too scrawny to keep," Lowdermilk explained.

A DEAD GIVEAWAY

When Jerry Glanville coached the Houston Oilers from 1985 through 1989, he had a habit of leaving free tickets at the Will Call window for the most lifeless people.

Actually, they were all dead.

For a 1988 preseason game in Memphis, he left a pass for the city's most famous celebrity, the late, great Elvis Presley. But The King was a no-show. So was actor James Dean, who died in 1955. Glanville had left a ticket for the Indiana native when the Oilers played the Indianapolis Colts.

In Dallas, the coach had a pass ready for Texas's long-gone favorite son, singer Buddy Holly.

And for a New York Jets game, he had a special sideline pass ready for the Phantom of the Opera.

FLIP FLOPS

Now that football is getting increasingly complicated, it's nice to watch the toss of the coin before every game. It's clean and simple. What could possibly go wrong? Plenty. Referees, players, and even movie stars have experienced great embarrassment during the traditional pregame ceremony. For "The Wackiest Coin Tosses Ever," The Football Hall of SHAME inducts the following:

ELIZABETH TAYLOR

Sept. 24, 1989

Elizabeth Taylor's mere presence on the field caused havoc during the coin toss of the Dallas Cowboys' home opener against the Washington Redskins in 1989.

Veteran NFL referee Pat Haggerty was so awestruck by Liz's presence that he allowed the actress to call the coin toss instead of rightfully giving the honor to the captains of the visiting Redskins.

Taylor joined the midfield ceremony as a guest of Cowboys owner Jerry Jones and she proceeded to make sane men goofy. Haggerty, who routinely faced down enraged, 300-pound linemen, turned into a puddle of mush when confronted with one of America's most glamorous movie stars.

The flustered ref first botched the introductions: "Dallas captains, meet the Washington captains; Washington captains, meet Liz Taylor and Jerry Jones . . . I mean, the Dallas captains."

Then, completely ignoring rules and tradition, Haggerty, by now as gaga as a starstruck teenager, invited Liz to call heads or tails.

"Heads," she said.

Heads it was and Haggerty awarded the ball to Dallas.

The official may have been in a trance, but the Redskins weren't blinded by the dazzling movie queen. With their coach, Joe Gibbs, screaming from the sidelines, the Washington captains told the ref, "Wait a minute. The visiting team gets to make the call."

Haggerty admitted his blunder. "You've got me all shook up," he told Taylor.

The Redskins won the second, legitimate, coin toss. They also won the game 30–7.

"You can see with Liz Taylor being there, I was a little nervous," an embarrassed Haggerty said later.

Coach Gibbs wasn't amused. "That's the first time I ever got mad at a coin flip," he grumbled.

TURK EDWARDS

Tackle ■ Washington Redskins ■ Sept. 22, 1940

Hall of Famer Turk Edwards became the first and only man in pro football history to be injured during, of all things, a coin-tossing ceremony.

Edwards—a tough, heady, agile tackle who played both offense and defense—was starting his ninth season in the NFL and his third with the Washington Redskins. As captain of the team, it was his job to take part in the coin flip.

Before the start of a 1940 game against the New York Giants, Edwards walked out to midfield where he met with the opposing captain, Mel Hein. The two hulking warriors were longtime friends from their undergraduate days together at Washington State. They exchanged pleasantries and then turned their attention to the referee.

The official pulled a silver dollar out of his pocket and flipped it. Hein called heads. It was tails. The Giants would kick off to the Redskins. The two players shook hands for what would be the last time at a coin toss.

"Good luck, Mel," said Edwards.

"Take care of yourself, Turk," said Hein. "Don't get hurt."

"Thanks, old buddy. I won't."

No sooner had Edwards uttered the words than he wheeled for the sideline and toppled over. His cleats had caught in the turf and when

he turned, he severely wrenched his knee. In fact, he was hurt so badly that he had to be carried off the field.

For Edwards, the pain was bad enough. But so was the embarrassment of getting hurt before a game. He assumed that his injury would heal in a week or so. But it never did.

The career of the seemingly indestructible tackle came crashing to an ironic end. The man who once missed only 10 minutes during an entire 12-game season was permanently put out of action not by a bruising opponent but by the most harmless part of a football game—the coin toss.

JERRY MARKBREIT

Referee ■ Jan. 28, 1983

Jerry Markbreit—one of the most respected referees in the NFL—waited until the eyes of the world were on him before screwing up in his first Super Bowl. His officiating was flawless. It was the coin toss that he botched.

"It was the most embarrassing, humiliating, horrifying moment of my career," he confessed. "It's also pretty amusing, but I'll never be able to laugh about it."

After officiating only seven seasons in the league, Markbreit had been rated number one by his peers and was selected to referee Super Bowl XVII in 1983. He was excited, honored—and nervous. Days before the big game, Markbreit had a premonition that he would flub the coin toss. "I was more worried about the toss than I was about the game."

At the Rose Bowl several hours before the game between the Miami Dolphins and the Washington Redskins, a league official told Markbreit that he would be using a special sterling-silver commemorative coin. Plans called for Hall of Famer Elroy "Crazy Legs" Hirsch to bring the coin to the middle of the field and give it to Markbreit. The ref wouldn't be able to see the coin before then. All he knew was the side of the coin with two helmets would be tails.

When the big moment arrived, Markbreit's knees wobbled and his heart pounded. He introduced the team captains, took the coin from

---

DON'T BET ON IT

Detroit Lions defensive tackle Alex Karras was suspended by the NFL for a year in 1963 for making a few friendly wagers.

A couple of years after his reinstatement, Karras was appointed co-captain. Moments before his first game as the team leader, he waddled to midfield for the traditional flipping of the coin.

"Captain Karras," said the referee. "I will toss the coin and while it is in the air, would you please call it heads or tails."

"I'm sorry, sir, but I can't," said Karras politely. "I'm not permitted to gamble."

Hirsch, and flipped it. According to Markbreit's book, *Born to Referee,* here's what happened next:

As the coin spun in the air, Dolphins captain Bob Kuechenberg called, "Tails!"

When it landed, Markbreit looked in the grass, saw those two helmets and, for some incomprehensible reason, announced, "Heads." He turned to Redskins captain Joe Theismann and said, "You win the toss." Hirsch tugged at the ref's shirt and whispered, "Jerry, I think the two helmets are tails."

Markbreit reached down and turned off his microphone, realizing that he had messed up the coin toss in front of one hundred million people. The flustered ref picked up the coin and looked at both sides. One side showed the two helmets and the other side had two players holding helmets.

Turning to Theismann, Markbreit, who was still in a fog, said, "It's heads. You still win the toss." Theismann shook his head and said, "Where the hell did they find you?"

Markbreit had become so confused and embarrassed at that point that he drew a complete blank. Finally, referee Dale Hamer came to the rescue. "What is tails?" he asked. Markbreit regained his senses and replied, "The two helmets." Hamer said, "Okay, it's tails. Miami wins the toss."

Recalled Markbreit: "I felt like crawling out of the stadium. If I could've disappeared and never officiated another game, I'd have done it. I was selected to work the biggest football game there is and I couldn't get by the coin toss."

ABNER HAYNES

Running Back ■ Dallas Texans ■ Dec. 23, 1962

Abner Haynes made the most shameful coin-toss decision in football history.

Given the choice of taking the wind or the football as his team prepared to enter a sudden-death overtime in the 1962 AFL championship game, Haynes ended up with neither!

Haynes, a running back for the Dallas Texans (forerunners of the Kansas City Chiefs), was the league's biggest star, having scored a record 19 touchdowns that year. Known as a smart and gifted player, the Dallas captain led his team into its biggest game ever against the Houston Oilers.

After racing out to a 17–0 halftime lead, with the help of two Haynes touchdowns, the Texans faltered. The Oilers roared back to tie the game at 17–17 before time ran out, forcing sudden-death overtime.

On the sidelines, before the toss of the coin for the overtime, Dallas coach Hank Stram sized up the situation with Haynes by his side. Strong, gusty winds were blowing toward a big clock at one end of Houston's Jeppesen Stadium. Stram was willing to give the Oilers first crack at the ball as long as the Texans would have the wind at their backs.

So the coach told Haynes, "If we win the toss, we want the wind. If they win the toss and elect to receive, we'll kick to the clock."

Haynes ran back onto the field and won the coin toss. It was his choice, so he told the referee, "We'll kick to the clock."

Incredibly, Haynes had blurted out his team's preference the wrong way! By using the words, "We'll kick," he had made his choice and had no say over which direction to kick. The Oilers captain quickly responded with, "We'll take the wind."

Thus Haynes, by an unbelievable blunder, had left the Texans with no advantage at all. They wouldn't be receiving the football and they wouldn't have the wind behind them. The players on the field, the fans in the stands, and the television viewers at home couldn't believe what Haynes had done. Neither could Stram, who turned white with shock.

"Abner should have simply said that we'd take the wind," the coach explained later. "He shouldn't have said anything about kicking."

Despite having the ball first and the wind at their backs as the overtime began, the Oilers failed to take advantage of Haynes's gaffe. The game went into a second overtime period which ended when Dallas kicker Tommy Brooker booted home a 25-yard field goal for a 20–17 Dallas victory.

Brooker was jubilant, Stram was thrilled, and the fans were ecstatic. But no one was happier than Abner Haynes.

BRAIN SPRAINS

Coaches and players commit to memory every detail of the game plan and playbook. They instantly size up the situation and know exactly what to do. Baloney! These guys daydream and get befuddled like the rest of us working stiffs. The only difference is that their office is the gridiron, and when they suffer a mental lapse, it usually spells disaster. For "The Most Mind-boggling Mental Miscues," The Football Hall of SHAME inducts the following:

JOHN ELWAY

Quarterback ■ Denver Broncos ■ Nov. 27, 1983

PHIL SIMMS

Quarterback ■ New York Giants ■ Oct. 23, 1988

Even though John Elway and Phil Simms have led their teams to the Super Bowl, both once lost their way on the gridiron during a game.

Each has felt the embarrassment of a quarterback's worst faux pas—lining up for the snap over the guard instead of the center.

It happened to Elway in his rookie year in 1983 during a 31–7 blowout of Denver by the Chargers in San Diego. Elway was harassed all day by the blitzing Chargers defense, which sacked him four times and snared three interceptions.

Things went from terrible to horrible to downright laughable by the fourth quarter. Trying to salvage a little dignity, the young quarterback directed the Broncos on one last drive with a hurry-up offense. But

Elway was so concerned about the rush that midway in the drive he set up behind left guard Tom Glassic and prepared to take the snap.

"He had his hands under me and I was trying to kick his foot with mine to tell him he was in the wrong place," Glassic recalled. "I was already in a set position so I couldn't move. But I bobbed my head and wiggled my ass and shouted, 'Hey, John, wrong guy! I don't have the ball!' "

Meanwhile, center Billy Bryan, who did have the ball, yelled at Elway, "Over here! Over here!"

A mortified Elway then scooted over behind the center, took the snap, and threw a pass out of bounds because he was so rattled. After the game, he told reporters with a sheepish smile, "At first I couldn't figure out what was wrong. I looked down and saw [tight end] John Sawyer just one person away and I couldn't figure out why Sawyer was there."

Added Glassic, "It's understandable how it could happen. All of us linemen have big rear ends, so it was easy to mistake one for another. Looking back on it, it was a disastrous day. But if you don't laugh, you cry."

At least Elway was a rookie when he tried to take a snap under the guard. Phil Simms (lower photo on left) was a 10-year veteran when he did the same thing in 1988—a year after leading the New York Giants to victory in Super Bowl XXI.

Simms' most embarrassing moment happened late in a tight game against the Atlanta Falcons. He went into a shotgun formation on third and eight on the Giants 10-yard line.

"I was looking to see what kind of coverage they had," Simms recalled. "I was really intense because we needed to score. Then I noticed what I thought was our guard waving his hand behind his back at me. I couldn't understand what he was doing. I mean, he was frantic.

"Then it dawned on me that our guard was really my center and that I had lined up over the right guard. I quickly moved over. But I was so flustered that I couldn't even remember what play I had called in the huddle. So when I got the snap, I just threw it to the first guy I saw open and by some miracle he caught it for a first down."

Center Bart Oates said he will never forget Simms' gaffe. "I was looking up the field to check out the defense and potential rushers," he recalled. "Phil was going into his cadence and I felt something wasn't quite right. I couldn't pinpoint it at first. Then I looked under my legs and I didn't see Phil. So I turned to my left and he wasn't there either. Then I looked to my right and I saw that he was standing behind our right guard, Eric Moore."

Oates tried waving his hand between his legs as discreetly as he could. But Simms didn't see him. Simms was too focused on looking over the Falcons' coverage.

It was almost time to snap the ball. So Oates turned around, still keeping his hands on the ball, and shouted, "Phil!" Finally, Simms moved over.

"I wouldn't have snapped the ball because he wouldn't have been expecting it from that angle," said Oates. "The ball would've either flown past him or it would've hit him.

"In the huddle after the play, I smiled at Phil and all he said was, 'Shut up.' Then he broke into a smile, too."

After the game, which the Giants won 23–16, Simms was hoping to forget his screwup. But it was not to be. "When I got home that night and turned on the TV, what do I see on the highlight film? Me lining up behind the guard. It was CNN's Play of the Day. I remember thinking, 'Man, isn't this a crock.' "

KEN STABLER

Quarterback ■ Alabama Crimson Tide ■ Oct. 16, 1965

Ken Stabler left his brains on the bench in the final seconds of a big game and cost Alabama a crucial victory over Tennessee.

The Crimson Tide had to settle for a 7–7 tie with the underdog Volunteers.

As a sophomore, Stabler began the season all pumped up because coach Bear Bryant had assigned him jersey number 12, the same numeral previously worn by Alabama football heroes Pat Trammell and Joe Namath. But Stabler played most of the season as a backup in the shadow of starter Steve Sloan.

Stabler, who emerged as one of the NFL's brainiest slingers, tossed only about a dozen passes in his sophomore year because Bryant used him mainly to run out the clock.

But against Tennessee, Stabler got the chance to show his stuff with some dramatic last-second heroics. What he showed instead was an embarrassing mental lapse that turned the Bear into a raging grizzly.

Late in the game with the score tied 7–7, Bryant sent Stabler in to replace Sloan, who was having a rare off day. With less than a minute remaining, the Tide launched a last-ditch drive with Stabler calling his own plays.

Using up all its timeouts, 'Bama drove to a first and goal just inside the Vols' 10-yard line. Fullback Steve Bowman then picked up two yards on a line plunge. But Stabler, attempting to pitch out on second down, was thrown for a 10-yard loss back to the 18-yard line. On third down, Stabler scrambled 14 yards to the 4-yard line, but he failed to get out of bounds to stop the clock.

Ten seconds remained—not enough time to get the field goal unit onto the field for an attempt at a game-winning kick. However, there still was time for one more play.

With fourth down and no timeouts left, everyone in the stadium knew it had to be a paydirt-or-bust play. Everyone, that is, but Stabler. He hurried his team to the line of scrimmage, took the snap—and deliberately threw the ball out of bounds!

Incredibly, Stabler mistakenly had thought it was only third down and that he had saved the day by stopping the clock with only six seconds remaining. Not until he saw the referee signal first down for Tennessee did Stabler realize he had blundered on fourth down and had killed the Tide's last chance to win. The game ended one play later in a tie.

PASS IMPERFECT

Diminutive Houston Oilers kicker Tony Zendejas proved that he didn't know how to throw his own weight around, let alone a football.

In a 1989 game against the Miami Dolphins, Zendejas was set to attempt a 35-yard field goal. But when holder Greg Montgomery dropped the snap, Zendejas wound up with the ball.

Fearing he'd get crushed by the onrushing linemen, Zendejas panicked. He threw a wounded duck in the air to no one in particular and it was intercepted by Miami's Louis Oliver. Fortunately, Houston overcame Zendejas' blunder and won the game.

"I was screaming for help, but I didn't see anybody," recalled Zendejas. "I figured I would get killed, so I threw the ball. I got killed anyway. I should have kept the ball."

The Alabama fans were in a state of shock. John Forney, who broadcast the Crimson Tide games on radio, said that when Stabler took the final snap and threw the ball out of bounds, "I stood up and screamed in the microphone, 'Wait!' I knew what he was going to do, but I couldn't stop him. I knew it was over."

The Alabama trainer, Jim Goostree, said the Tennessee players were deliriously happy with the outcome. "They shook hands with Stabler and thanked him," Goostree recalled.

A mortified Stabler trudged to the sideline to face the wrath of Coach Bryant. "Stabler!" shouted the coach. "Have you lost your mind?"

"He was furious," Stabler later recalled. "I had helped give Tennessee, not a strong team at the time, a major moral victory."

When the Alabama players reached the dressing room, the door was locked. Stabler learned firsthand that it wasn't wise to irritate the Bear. Instead of waiting for the key, Bryant ordered Alabama State Trooper Joe Smelley to shoot the lock off the door.

Smelley declined, fearing the ricochet would kill three or four bystanders.

"Well, then, get your fat fanny out of the way," the Bear growled. Bryant then delivered a forearm smash that knocked the door off the hinges.

JIM MARSHALL

Defensive End ■ Minnesota Vikings ■ Oct. 25, 1964

No player in NFL history ever lost his direction more shamefully than Jim Marshall did. He picked up a fumble and rambled 62 yards into the end zone. Unfortunately, it was the wrong one.

Marshall thought he had scored a touchdown for his team. But because he went this-a-way when he should have gone that-a-way, he actually had scored a safety for his opponents.

"You can imagine how it was for me," he said later. "I have never been so humiliated."

Marshall—a five-year pro and member of the Minnesota Vikings' famed defensive line, the Purple People Eaters—was playing his heart out in a game against the 49ers in San Francisco's Kezar Stadium.

Early in the fourth quarter with the Vikings leading 27–17, the 49ers were on the move at their own 38-yard line.

Quarterback George Mira dropped back and, with the onrushing Marshall in pursuit, dumped a swing pass to running back Billy Kilmer. At the line of scrimmage, Kilmer was hit so hard that he fumbled. Marshall, having rushed the passer, turned around and scooped up the loose ball. Then, without hesitation, he sprinted for what he thought was the Minnesota goal line.

Marshall zipped past several startled and momentarily confused players and then broke into the open. He left behind his pursuers—who weren't the 49ers but his own teammates. They yelled at him to stop, but the roar from the crowd drowned out their shouts. Meanwhile, his teammates on the sidelines were running beside him stride for stride, screaming at him, too.

"I thought they were cheering for me," said Marshall. "About the five-yard line, I looked around and things just didn't seem right." For one thing, the hometown fans were cheering, and the Vikings were the visiting team.

As Marshall crossed the goal line, he noticed Minnesota quarterback Fran Tarkenton yelling at him from the sidelines and pointing in the opposite direction. "I couldn't think of anything else to do, so I threw him the ball," said Marshall.

Because Marshall was already in his own end zone when he threw the ball out of bounds, the refs ruled the play a safety. His blunder could have been worse. Had the ball landed within the end zone, the 49ers would have had a chance to recover it for a touchdown. Nevertheless, San Francisco picked up two gift points to make the score 27–19.

Marshall still didn't realize what he had done—but he knew whatever it was, it was wrong. San Francisco center Bruce Bosley was the first 49er to reach Marshall in the end zone. Bosley threw his arms around him and thanked him for the safety. "I told Jim, 'Thanks a lot. We can use more of those.' He just looked at me like I was off my rocker and said, 'Huh?' Then he looked up in the stands and then at the sidelines with a strange look in his eye. I don't think it was until he had walked 20 yards that he knew what had happened."

That's when Tarkenton ran up to Marshall and said, "Jim, you went the wrong way! The wrong way!"

Marshall buried his head in his hands for a few anguished moments and then jogged back to the bench. Coach Norm Van Brocklin, a man with a notoriously short temper, chose not to berate his mortified player. Instead, the coach smacked Marshall on the rear and said, "Forget about it, Jim. Go back in there and make the fans forget."

Marshall played just as hard as always and despite his screwup, the Vikings held on for a 27–22 victory. Only then did they all laugh about his wrong-way run—even Marshall. When he got off the team plane in Minneapolis later that night, he told the press, "All the guys on the plane asked me to take over as pilot. They figured I'd land them in Hawaii."

Within days, Marshall had received hundreds of letters from fans, most advising him not to let his blunder get him down. One of the letters came from Roy Riegels, who 35 years earlier had etched his name in college football history as the No. 1 bonehead of all time. Playing for California in the 1929 Rose Bowl, Riegels ran nearly 70 yards the wrong way, which led directly to his team's 8–7 defeat.

Riegels, who advised Marshall that the best thing to do was laugh about his mistake, began his letter with the words, "Welcome to the club!"

BOB DICKINSON   JOE SETRON

Fullback ■ Rutgers   Guard ■ West Virginia

CHARLEY HOWARD

Tackle ■ West Virginia
Oct. 28, 1922

Bob Dickinson, Joe Setron, and Charley Howard collaborated on a blunderfully wrong-way play that nearly equaled the classic gridiron gaffes of Roy Riegels and Jim Marshall.

But at least Riegels and Marshall each achieved infamy by himself. It took three chowderheaded players to duplicate a similar screwup during the West Virginia Mountaineers' 28–0 drubbing of the Rutgers Scarlet Knights in 1922.

Late in the second quarter, Dickinson, playing defense for Rutgers, dove into a pileup at the Scarlet Knights' 43-yard line and saw the ball pop loose from the Mountaineer running back. Quick as a flash, Dickinson grabbed the pigskin and started upfield. Desperately wanting to score for the underdog Knights, he put his head down and aimed for the goal line. He bounced off one tackler and was hit by another at the West Virginia 35-yard line.

But Dickinson was spun around and, in his confusion, started running in the wrong direction toward his own goal line!

With a clear field ahead of him, the mixed-up Dickinson should have crossed the opponent's goal line with ease. Except that West Virginia's Joe Setron and Charley Howard were just as mixed up as he was.

"There he goes!" yelled Setron.

"Let's get him!" shouted Howard.

"No, don't!" hollered the rest of the Mountaineers. But their pleas were too late. Setron and Howard set out in hot pursuit of the wrong-way runner. It looked like a scene out of a Keystone Cops movie. While Setron and Howard were chasing Dickinson, their own teammates were chasing them.

Finally, after a 25-yard pursuit, the two wayward Mountaineers caught up with the wayward Dickinson and tackled him at the Rutgers 32-yard line. As Setron and Howard lay on the ground congratulating themselves, their teammates rushed up to them and gave them hell.

SACK IT TO ME

Miami Dolphins quarterback Bob Griese holds the dubious distinction of losing the most yardage on a sack in Super Bowl history—an incredible 29 yards!

In the second quarter of Super Bowl VI, the Hall of Famer dropped back to pass and was pursued by Dallas Cowboys defensive tackles Bob Lilly and Jethro Pugh. Like a chased cat, Griese turned tail and scampered left and right, then backtracked and zigzagged until he was finally brought down by an out-of-breath Lilly.

"We could have finished this a whole lot sooner," said Lilly, still huffing and puffing, "if you had cooperated and just fallen down."

"I would have," said an equally exhausted Griese, "if I had known you could run that far."

"What are you sore about?" Setron snapped back. "We tackled him, didn't we?"

"That's why we're sore," said a furious Mountaineer teammate. "You tackled a guy who was running in the wrong direction! If you would've just left him alone, he would have run right into his end zone and we would've scored at least a safety."

Dickinson rose to his feet and, while hiding his own embarrassment, decided to shame his two tacklers. "Hey," he told them, "thanks for helping me out. I would've really looked like a fool if I had made it all the way to the end zone. But you guys were even bigger fools for tackling me."

TOM GLASSIC

Offensive Guard ■ Denver Broncos ■ Jan. 15, 1978

Tom Glassic was late for the biggest game of his life—Super Bowl XII—because he was asleep when the team bus left.

"You dream your whole life of playing in the Super Bowl and then when you're one of the lucky few who actually gets to be in one, you show up late," said Glassic, who was the starting left guard for the Denver Broncos in the 1978 Super Bowl clash with the Dallas Cowboys.

Before the game at the Superdome in New Orleans, Glassic decided to take a little nap in the hotel room of his parents, John and Margaret. The respite lasted longer than he had planned. While Glassic was snoozing, the three team buses pulled out of the hotel entrance for the 45-minute drive to the Superdome.

"Hey, Tom," said his dad, peering out the window. "Isn't that your bus?"

Glassic bolted out of bed and rushed to the window just as the third bus drove off. "Oh, no!" he moaned. "That's my bus leaving."

Glassic raced down to the lobby and out the door, frantically trying to find a fast way to get to the game. "I ran up to a policeman and pleaded with him to give me a ride in his squad car," recalled Glassic. "I told him who I was and that I was playing in the Super Bowl. But he didn't believe me at first. Finally, the families of the players and my parents crowded around and convinced the cop that I was really a Denver Bronco who had missed the bus." By the time Glassic hopped in the squad car, traffic had slowed to a crawl. "Unfortunately, the traffic was real heavy and the cop took his sweet time in getting me to the Superdome. He was casually talking about the point spread and how the teams matched up, things like that. Man, my stomach was all twisted in knots."

But Glassic's worries weren't over once he arrived at the Superdome. There was the problem of how to get in. "The cop dropped me off and drove on. So here I was at the gate dressed in jeans and a sweatshirt and I'm telling the security guard that I need to get in there because I'm playing in the Super Bowl. To make matters worse, I don't have any identification on me or a player's pass."

Naturally, the security guard didn't believe him. Glassic begged. He pleaded. He shouted. Finally, after 15 frustrating minutes, he persuaded the guard to send someone into the Denver locker room to summon help. An assistant equipment manager returned and vouched for Glassic.

But the tardy Bronco had one more hurdle to clear—getting by his coach, Red Miller. "Wouldn't you know that Red was standing outside the locker room door when I came in," said Glassic. "So I went past him and said, 'Sorry about that, Coach.' He had his arms folded and he stared at me with an awful look and then just shook his head. He didn't say a word."

Once inside, Glassic had to face a few razzberries from his teammates. "Glad you could make it, Tom," said a Bronco. Added another player, "We heard you were overmatched at your position, but we didn't think you'd be afraid to show up."

Because he was so late, Glassic rushed to get taped up and put on his uniform. "Before every sporting event that I ever participated in, I always threw up. But not this time. I was so nervous that I *didn't* puke."

Glassic wasn't fined for being late, but he almost wished he had been. "I think the only reason I wasn't fined was that it was so insignificant compared to what happened in the game," he said. Denver was crushed 27–10.

BOB FENIMORE

Tailback ■ Oklahoma A & M Aggies ■ Oct. 7, 1944

Ball carrier Bob Fenimore belly flopped his way into The Football Hall of SHAME when he leaped for the goal line—and came up 10 yards short!

During a night game against Texas Tech in Lubbock, Texas, Fenimore dove for what he thought was a go-ahead touchdown to climax a sensational 45-yard dash.

But when he looked around, the mortified Aggie found himself on his belly just inside the 10-yard line while a pursuing Tech Red Raider was convulsed with laughter. Fenimore had mistaken the yard marker for the end-zone line and his dramatic lunge for the touchdown turned into a daffy dive that left him high and dry.

What made the blunder even more embarrassing was that Fenimore earned All-America honors that same season and again the following year, and led the nation in offense both seasons.

"I doubt if I would have made All-America in 1944 if the people who voted for me had seen me make that dive," laughed Fenimore.

"I was very embarrassed. Most people, including my coach and my teammates, thought I had tripped over my own big feet. It was a long time before I told anyone the truth."

Fenimore said the field at Lubbock was poorly lighted and the yard markers were not as distinctive as they are today. Both factors, he said, contributed to his abbreviated run to pay dirt.

The score was knotted at 7–7 late in the game when Fenimore took a handoff deep in his own territory, squirted through the line, and broke free into the secondary. A single Red Raider stayed on his heels as Fenimore sprinted downfield.

"I knew how important a touchdown was," Fenimore recalled. "The Texas Tech man was breathing down my neck. I wanted to make sure I scored so when I got to what I thought was the goal line, I made that big old high dive. I lay there with a big grin on my face. I thought I had won the game."

Not quite. The Red Raider in pursuit wore an even bigger grin when he caught up to Fenimore. As he stood over the prone runner, the laughing defender pointed at the goal line 10 yards away and crowed: "You missed!"

Much to Fenimore's relief, the Aggies scored the winning touchdown a few plays later.

"We won the game 14–7," said Fenimore. "I got the touchdown and I made darn sure I was over the goal line before I celebrated the second time. I guarantee you, after that I always made sure I knew where I was on the field."

TACKLING DUMMIES

Hall of Famers Jim Thorpe and Joe Guyon of the Canton Bulldogs planned to ambush hated rival Fritz Pollard of the Akron Pros in a 1920 game.

The two Bulldogs told their punter to kick the ball high and short to Pollard. The plan called for Thorpe and Guyon to rush downfield, blindside Pollard from opposite directions just as he received the punt, and knock him out of the game.

The scheme almost worked. Pollard caught the ball and Thorpe and Guyon converged on him with flying tackles. But the cagey Pollard ducked at the last second and the two charging Bulldogs smashed into each other in a violent collision that left both sprawled unconscious on the ground.

When they were revived, the dazed duo were too wobbly to play for the rest of the first half. Without their full services, Canton lost 7–0.

BILL CHIPLEY

Defensive End ■ Washington & Lee Generals ■ Oct. 12, 1946

Washington & Lee defensive end Bill Chipley got so confused after taking a hard hit that he huddled up with the wrong team—the West Virginia Mountaineers.

By the time they finished counting noses and sent Chipley back to the right huddle, the Mountaineers were slapped with a delay of game penalty that nearly cost them the game.

West Virginia probably would have spotted Chipley in their huddle a lot quicker had not all the players been caked with mud. Heavy rains had turned the field in Charleston into a soggy, muddy mess.

"By the end of the first quarter, it was hard to tell which side was which," said Chipley. "Players from both teams were the same color—mud brown from head to toe."

Early in the fourth quarter of a scoreless tie, West Virginia finally threatened. The Mountaineers moved the ball to the Generals' 5-yard line and, on fourth and goal, decided to go for the touchdown.

But on the previous play, Chipley had taken a hard blow to the head. He got to his feet and staggered dizzily over to the Mountaineers' huddle instead of joining his own teammates.

"I just kind of wandered into their huddle, shaking my head trying to clear the cobwebs," Chipley recalled. "I remember hearing the quarterback call some strange-sounding play that didn't make any sense to me.

"Just as they were ready to break the huddle, I held up my hand and said, 'Check that. I don't know that play. What am I supposed to do?'"

Chipley's newfound "teammates" tried to explain, but the dazed General kept shaking his head. And the harder they tried, the angrier they became.

Time was running out when the West Virginia back, whose play had just been called, suddenly realized there were too many Mountaineers in one place. Frantically, they scraped the mud off one another until they uncovered the interloper.

"Someone yelled at me, 'What the hell are you doing here?'" Chipley laughed. "All I said was 'Oops!' and then tried to sneak back to my own side of the line.

"About that time, the referee blew his whistle on West Virginia for delay of game. That really drove them wild. They argued it wasn't their fault, but the ref still marked off the 5-yard penalty."

The penalty hurt because the Mountaineers failed to score from the 10-yard line on fourth and goal. The Generals took over on downs. However, West Virginia did manage to score a touchdown in the waning seconds of the game to eke out a 6–0 victory—but only after counting everyone in the huddle twice before running the winning play.

SCHOOL DAZE

During the 1965 season, the Green Bay Packers fell into a terrible slump, scoring only 36 points in four games.

Coach Vince Lombardi called the offensive team together, then announced that he must be a terrible teacher because they had forgotten everything he had taught them.

"We're going back to basics," said Lombardi. "Back to fundamentals." He paused and then picked up a ball. "This," he announced sarcastically, "is a football."

"Hold on, Coach," said wide receiver Max McGee from the back of the room. "You're going too fast."

SICK KICKS

Kickers think of themselves as game-winners who have the fate of their teams riding on their talented toes. But sometimes their fortunes are more like bad punts—shanked out of bounds. To the lousy kicker, hang time means how long it will take for irate fans to string him up, and the coffin corner is where they want to bury him. For "The Most Inept Kicking Performances," The Football Hall of SHAME inducts the following:

JAY ESTABROOK

Punter ■ Tufts Jumbos ■ Oct. 29, 1965

RON WIDBY

Punter ■ Dallas Cowboys ■ Sept. 21, 1969

Kickers Jay Estabrook and Ron Widby share a special niche reserved for the most pitiful punts ever booted. They each caught their own punts!

For Jay Estabrook, of Tufts University, it was a punter's worst nightmare come true. He watched horrified as his feeble kick rose into a brisk breeze—and floated right back into his arms.

"I was standing there with my mouth open, trying to wave it away," Estabrook said. "I didn't want to catch it. I wasn't supposed to catch it. Other people were supposed to catch my punts. Not me!"

Estabrook's embarrassing kick hurt both his ego and his team's chances in a 1965 game against Amherst College. The backward punt resulted in a 4-yard loss and set up a touchdown for the Lord Jeffs.

The Tufts Jumbos were playing at Amherst's Pratt Field, where stiff, 25-mile-an-hour gusts were whipping right down the center of the exposed field.

"There were just bare wooden bleachers along the sidelines and nothing in the end zones to block the wind," Estabrook recalled. "And for kickers, the wind is your worst enemy. I never thought much about getting blocked, but I sure hated to kick when it was windy."

In the second quarter, with Tufts on its own 15-yard line, the reluctant punter had to go in and kick directly into the wind.

"I didn't get much of a spiral on the ball," Estabrook explained. "In fact, I didn't get any. It was just one of those weak, fluttery little kicks that you want to turn your back on and pretend that somebody else booted it.

"The ball crossed the line of scrimmage, so technically I couldn't have kicked it again when I 'received' it even if I wanted to.

"Everyone else was dashing madly downfield, but I stood there watching the punt go up in the air and then come sailing right back in my direction. I was the only one left in the neighborhood and to my surprise, and everyone else's in the stands, the ball came right to me."

The perplexed punter stood transfixed for a few seconds, cradling the ball. Just as Estabrook took a few tentative steps, an Amherst player spotted the shameful punt and dashed back to tackle the kicker.

It ended up being a 4-yard loss and Amherst took over on downs at the Tufts' 11-yard line. The Lord Jeffs eventually scored on the turnover and ended up dumping the Jumbos 28–6.

Four years later, Dallas Cowboys punter Ron Widby nearly duplicated Estabrook's bumbling boot in a game at the Cotton Bowl. But since he was a pro, Widby didn't suffer the ignominious 4-yard loss the amateur Estabrook did. Widby fielded the ball after it traveled a measly eight yards, making him perhaps the only punter in the NFL to catch his own kick.

"Every kicker gets off some dumb boots in his career, but that was definitely my worst one," recalled Widby. "I know for sure it was the one that embarrassed me the most.

"The Cowboys were still playing in the Cotton Bowl at the time and those Texas breezes can get pretty stiff. But that was only part of the problem. I just plain squibbed the kick."

The Cowboys were stampeding the St. Louis Cardinals 24–3 when Widby's punt left him in shame.

"Nobody was rushing me," he recalled. "I had plenty of time, but I blew it. The ball went off the side of my foot and started taking all kinds of crazy bounces.

"You couldn't tell where the ball was going. The guys from both teams were jumping around trying to stay out of its way. Nobody wanted to down the ball before they knew what direction it was going to take.

"I kind of ran up to the line of scrimmage after I punted the ball and was standing there watching the action. I couldn't believe I had booted one that bad."

Widby not only forgot how to kick, he forgot how to dodge. While he stood there watching the bouncing ball, it suddenly rebounded straight at him.

"The next thing I knew, I was holding the damn thing," said Widby. "I just stumbled forward and downed it. That was the only time I ever caught my own punt. I made sure it was the last time."

JIM HOGAN

Punter ■ Central Florida Knights ■ Nov. 15, 1986

For the final game of his college career, University of Central Florida punter Jim Hogan said he wanted to be remembered for something different.

Hogan got his wish—but it wasn't exactly what he had in mind. Late in the game, he took his final snap from center and then stunned the crowd. Rather than kick the ball away, Hogan bowed to the spectators on the left, bowed to the ones on the right, and bowed to the fans in each end zone.

Unfortunately, he took so long bowing that when he finally got around to booting his final punt, it was blocked and returned for a touchdown!

The week before the game against Samford University, Hogan announced that to cap his football career, he would punt backward and boot the ball out of his own end zone. Then he changed his mind and settled on a princely bow to the crowd. Recalled Hogan:

"We knew we would win by a big score, so when Coach [Gene McDowell] heard what I was planning, he told me not to do it. He said it would just be rubbing it in.

"In the fourth quarter we were ahead 66–0 and I went out to punt.

I knew it would be my very last one. When I got the snap, I just held the ball, turned in all four directions, and waved and bowed to all the people who were there.

"Then I started to punt. I had some friends up in the crowd and I was going to kick it to them, but it was blocked before I got it away and Samford took it in for a touchdown to make the final score 66–7. I was extremely embarrassed because we lost the shutout, which would have been our first in years."

But Hogan didn't hang around to hear the groans of disappointment. Rather than face the wrath of Coach McDowell, Hogan sprinted straight to the tunnel in the stadium, quickly changed, jumped in his car, and sped away with six minutes still remaining on the game clock.

It meant only a single touchdown in Central Florida's meaningless blowout over Samford, but the stunt cost Hogan more than a little loss of face.

"I had been telling everybody all week long I was going to do it," Hogan said. "But the coach didn't have a sense of humor. He took away my scholarship."

GREG GANTT

Punter ■ Alabama Crimson Tide ■ Dec. 2, 1972

Greg Gantt and his Alabama teammates literally kicked away their big game against arch rival Auburn on back-to-back blocked punts in the final minutes of the contest.

In 1972, the undefeated Crimson Tide, ranked No. 2 in the nation with a 10–0–0 record, held a seemingly comfortable 16–3 lead over the Tigers late in the fourth quarter. But suddenly the tide turned against the Tide.

With 5:30 left, Alabama went into punt formation on the 50-yard line. Gantt took the snap and drove his kick right into the hands of Auburn linebacker Bill Newton. The ball ricocheted past Gantt, hit the ground, and bounced into the grasp of defender David Langner at the 25-yard line. Langner then scampered untouched into the end zone for a touchdown. The extra point sliced the Tide's margin to 16–10.

On its next possession, 'Bama managed to hold on to the ball for about four minutes before the Tigers again held on downs and forced

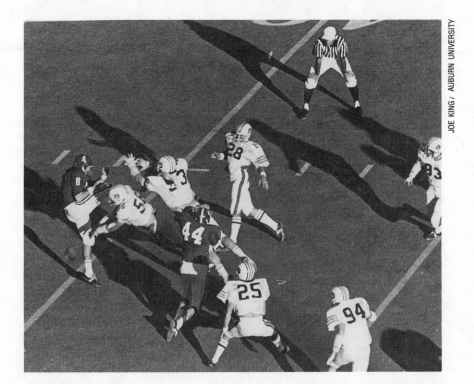

Gantt to punt from his 43-yard line. Fans at Jordan Hare Stadium in Auburn, Alabama, who might have missed the lightning-quick score off Gantt's last punt attempt, had a chance to witness a real-life instant replay.

With only 1:34 remaining, Gantt tried to nail a booming punt that would pin the Tigers deep in their own territory. But once again, he booted the ball right into the hands of a leaping Bill Newton. And once again, David Langner was right there. He scooped up the ball at the 'Bama 20-yard line and ran it in unscathed for the tying touchdown.

The stadium rocked with pandemonium as Auburn's Gardner Jett kicked the extra point to vault the Tigers into a 17–16 lead. About 36,000 fans erupted in joyous hysteria while another 36,000 on the other side sat in shocked silence.

"The bad thing was you could sense the second blocked kick before it happened," recalled 'Bama defensive back Jeff Blitz. "We were on the sidelines scurrying around trying to make adjustments, but we didn't have time. The whole thing happened so damn fast. They blocked one and then . . . boom . . . they blocked another kick. I was in a state of disbelief."

Having blown a sure victory on Gantt's two blocked punts, Alabama was too stunned to rally and lost 17–16. Just to rub salt into the wound, thousands of auto and truck bumpers in Alabama were quickly adorned with orange and blue stickers that read, "PUNT, 'BAMA, PUNT."

The staggering upset so demoralized coach Bear Bryant's boys that they also lost to Texas 17–13 a month later in the Cotton Bowl and blew any chance of a national championship.

"The Cotton Bowl was over before we even got to Dallas," recalled Blitz. "We were so depressed after Auburn beat us that we couldn't concentrate on getting up for Texas.

"The Auburn game is something we'll live with the rest of our lives.

"Auburn won't let us forget. I still see those 'PUNT, 'BAMA, PUNT' bumper stickers."

THE JAKAWENKO BROTHERS

Aug. 12, 1974

Two Czech brothers conned Kansas City Chiefs coach Hank Stram into signing up one of them as a kicker.

During the 1974 preseason, NFL players went on strike and left the teams to cope with rookies and walk-ons. One of those walk-ons was Jaroslav Jakawenko, who showed up at the Buffalo Bills training camp and asked coach Lou Saban for a tryout.

"In those days, we'd give anybody a tryout and with the strike going on as well, we were so desperate we'd sign up anyone who even recognized a football," Saban said. "Also, the sidewinders were just coming into vogue and every team in the league wanted a soccer-style kicker.

"So when this Czech guy showed up and said he was a kicker, I figured he had to be good if he was a sidewinder. Except he was terrible, so I sent him on his way."

Jakawenko then negotiated by telephone to kick for the Kansas City Chiefs. However, he had a sudden change of heart and decided to hang up his cleats for good. So instead of heading west to join the Chiefs, the kicker sent his brother, Ludvik.

When Ludvik Jakawenko arrived in Kansas City sight unseen,

Coach Stram handed him a uniform and a kicking tee, thinking he was Jaroslav Jakawenko.

Two weeks later, Buffalo came to Kansas City for an exhibition game. During the pregame warmup, Saban noticed the Jakawenko name on the roster, but when he watched the kicker practice, Saban didn't recognize him as the same one he'd cut.

"The guy was at least 50 pounds heavier than the one who tried out for me," Saban recalled. "I went over to Stram and asked him what they'd been feeding that guy. It looked like they'd pumped him up with a bicycle pump. And he couldn't kick worth a damn either!"

Saban then realized that the brothers had pulled a fast one on Kansas City. He roared with laughter and told Stram, "You've been scammed."

"Hank screamed bloody murder," Saban recalled. "He started yelling, 'I've been had!' and bouncing up and down. About that time the game started, and Stram couldn't do anything about it."

But at halftime, Stram stormed into the locker room and cut Jakawenko on the spot.

Stram admitted he'd been hoodwinked by the Jakawenko brothers. "I still don't know who they were," he said years later. "You know how it is with those Czechoslovakian names. They all sound alike."

HEADLESS COACHES

Those who can, do. Those who can't, teach. Those who can't do either, coach. And sometimes they don't do that very well. The lucky ones can mishandle players, draw up a crummy game plan, call the wrong plays, and still win because they have the talented players. But even if they try hard to hide behind their won-lost record, their goofs and gaffes become glaring enough for all to see. For "The Most Foolish Actions of Coaches," The Football Hall of SHAME inducts the following:

MIKE DITKA

Coach ■ Chicago Bears ■ 1987

The mouth of Chicago Bears coach Mike Ditka once got him into trouble with the league and the law. It wasn't the words that he spewed; it was the spit.

In 1987, the tempestuous coach led the league in unspitsmanlike conduct.

First, there was the ExpectorGate scandal. During a game against the Minnesota Vikings, Ditka let fly with a gob that landed on head linesman Earnie Frantz, who had flagged Chicago tackle Keith Van Horne for a false start.

Ditka ranted and raved over the call. Frantz chose to ignore the temper tantrum until he felt a few drops upon his face. Since the game was played indoors at the Metrodome, the ref concluded that the shower came not from God but straight from the coach's mouth. Ditka's indiscretion cost his team a 15-yard penalty and triggered an NFL investigation into what became known as "The Tempest in a Spittoon." The results of the probe were kept confidential.

Bears special teams coach Steve Kazor came to Ditka's defense in a left-handed way. He claimed that Mike didn't really mean to spit at the ref. Instead, said Kazor, Ditka had been a victim of his own inexperience as a tobacco chewer. "I didn't see him spit at the official. Mike had tobacco juice slobbering down his face. He was misjudged because he was an amateur tobacco chewer."

Quarterback Jim McMahon, a spitting image of an expert chewer, admitted that Ditka's expectoration "was a pretty weak effort."

That wasn't the first time the fiery coach had suffered a bad case of the spits. Recalled backup quarterback Jim Harbaugh, "At Denver, he went after this one official and spit gum right in his ear."

Things got a little sticky for Ditka the week after the Minnesota mess when the bears were slaughtered by the San Francisco 49ers 41–0 at Candlestick Park.

On the way to the locker room at halftime, the Bears had to run a gauntlet of jeering 49er fans who were throwing ice and debris at the players. Ditka gestured to the fans (see photo), singled out a target, and let fly with a thick wad of green gum that he had been chewing. It struck Terry Ornelas, 38, of Napa, California, in the back of the head and stuck in her hair. She immediately complained to police.

San Francisco cop George Pohley filed this report: "As I was escorting Coach Ditka from the playing field, he stopped and looked at the people sitting in the pullout seats. He then took a piece of gum from his mouth and threw it at victim-reportee Ornelas, striking her in the back of the head. Coach Ditka then flipped the bird and exited the field."

Ornelas didn't press charges, although she said she thought Ditka owed her an apology and that the NFL should fine him for rudeness. "It's the principle of the thing," said her attorney, David Schotte. "My client was outraged."

Ditka said he threw the gum because fans pelted him with ice. "Any time somebody throws something at me, I'm going to throw something back," he declared.

The Gum Caper was front-page news in the morning editions of the *San Francisco Chronicle*. Even the police department got caught up in all the publicity. Many times the cops had shown off confiscated evidence like guns, knives, and drugs for the television cameras. But two days after the game, at the Hall of Justice, the police displayed the most notorious weapon of assault ever confiscated at a football game—Ditka's deadly wad of green gum.

DON SHULA

Defensive Coach ■ Detroit Lions ■ Aug. 14, 1960

Don Shula—one of the winningest head coaches in NFL history—launched his coaching career with an embarrassing game plan that left him shaken and shamefaced.

On the very first play he called as defensive coach for the Detroit Lions, the Cleveland Browns scored a touchdown!

Shula joined the Detroit coaching staff at the start of the 1960 season after an outstanding playing career as a defensive back. Head coach George Wilson gave Shula the job of calling the Lions' defensive plays from the press box.

When the first preseason game rolled around, Shula was ready. And a little excited. The Lions were facing the Browns—the team Shula had first broken in with as a player nine years earlier. He was anxious to demonstrate his coaching prowess to his former teammates.

For Shula, it was an inauspicious debut.

Cleveland's Willmer Fowler took the opening kickoff on his goal line and ran it back 60 yards to the Detroit 40-yard line. As Browns quarterback Milt Plum led his offensive unit onto the field, Shula took a deep breath. It was now up to the young coach to send down his first play ever for the Lions' defense.

Shula called for one-coverage, or a single coverage formation against the Cleveland receivers. But the Browns came out in an unexpected formation with wide receiver Ray Renfro lined up as the weakside tight end.

"As Renfro lined up, I could see that our secondary was a little confused as to what the coverage was supposed to be," recalled Shula.

But it was too late to make an adjustment. When the ball was snapped, Renfro cut over the middle and caught a perfectly thrown pass from Plum. There wasn't a Detroit defender in sight as Renfro raced untouched 40 yards for a touchdown on the first play from scrimmage.

"I almost fell out of the press box," admitted Shula.

He didn't have time to feel badly. He was too busy frantically trying to figure out a defensive scheme that would work as the Browns scored three touchdowns in the first 12 minutes of the game—in fact, the first three times they touched the ball. Detroit never recovered and lost 28–14.

Although today he's the winningest active coach in the NFL, Shula says, "I'll never forget the first play I was responsible for as a coach."

HERMAN HICKMAN

Assistant Coach ■ North Carolina State Wolfpack ■ Oct. 14, 1939

To fire his team up for a game against arch rival Wake Forest, North Carolina State assistant coach Herman Hickman mailed his players anonymous threatening letters and blamed Wake Forest for writing them.

But his scheme backfired. Instead of getting charged up and seeking vengeance, his players trembled in fear and the Wolfpack suffered their worst beating ever inflicted by the Demon Deacons.

"In 1939, our big game was with Wake Forest," Hickman recalled. "It was the one game that we wanted to win above all others."

Even though State regularly whipped Wake Forest, Hickman knew that opposing coach Peahead Walker was loaded with bruising, hulking players. During the previous two years, Walker had combed the coal-mining sections of Pennsylvania recruiting the biggest, meanest, toughest players he could find. "Peahead had reached the point where he didn't look natural unless he was wearing his carbide lamp on his cap because he had been going down into the coal mines," said Hickman.

"With those big players he had, I knew that some drastic measures had to be taken. So I hit on the idea of writing letters to all the boys on the North Carolina State squad in order to rouse them up for the game."

Hickman diligently wrote every member of the starting team a nasty, threatening, insulting letter. He warned the quarterback that he had better not show up Saturday unless he was planning on throwing the ball from a position flat on his back because that's where he was going to be. He wrote to the linemen and told them they better look at themselves in the mirror now or have their pictures taken before the game because they were not going to have any teeth left after the game. Hickman signed each letter "A Wake Forest Player."

To make the letters seem more real, he drove from the campus in Raleigh to Wake Forest and dropped the letters in the post office there so they would have the Wake Forest postmark on them.

"I sat back the rest of the week with confidence because I knew that our boys were going to be ready," the coach said.

If they were ready, it sure wasn't for football. To Hickman's shock and dismay, the Wolfpack took the letters to heart. By the time his players walked onto the field, they felt fearful and intimidated—and they played that way. The Demon Deacons rolled all over State in a stunning 32–0 drubbing.

The game showed Hickman that he possessed a hidden talent. "I didn't realize until then my literary prowess."

LOU SABAN

Coach ■ Buffalo Bills ■ Dec. 12, 1965

Buffalo Bills coach Lou Saban once tried a novel way of getting quarterback Jack Kemp's attention during halftime—Saban stuffed him in a locker!

The coach, fuming mad over the lackluster performance of his team, needed an excuse to fire up the players. So he decided to slam-dunk his 6-foot, 1-inch, 200-pound quarterback for disregarding instructions from the bench and calling his own plays during the first half.

Kemp, who quit football a few years later for a life in public service, was appointed secretary of the Department of Housing and Urban Development in 1989.

For the Bills, 1965 had been a very good year. They were on their way to the AFL championship with a 10–3–1 record. But as the season wound down, they still needed to win their last two games.

In the next to last game, Buffalo held a 20–7 lead over Kansas City at halftime. But Coach Saban was not a happy camper. The lifeless

Bills were not playing up to par and an independent-minded Kemp had ignored many of Saban's plays in favor of his own.

"When Saban got on a guy, he usually did it one on one so he didn't have to embarrass the player," recalled defensive end Tom Day. "But when we came in at halftime of the Chiefs' game, everybody could tell Lou was really pissed.

"The coach took Kemp over to one side and was reading him the riot act. All of a sudden we heard all this yelling and banging. Saban had picked up Kemp and shoved him into one of the lockers!"

Saban recalled that he intended to set Kemp straight on who called the plays for the team, but that the quarterback wanted to debate the point.

"I got a lot of 'But coach . . .' stuff from him," said Saban. "Finally, I ran out of patience. There was a vacant locker right there so I picked him up and shoved him into it. I tried to slam the door on him but his big butt was sticking out."

In the second half, Kemp followed orders to the letter and the Bills whipped the Chiefs 34–25.

"I never had much trouble with Jack after that," Saban said. "If he did start to give me any lip, I'd just point to a locker and ask him if he wanted to go back in there for a while."

SORRY, WRONG NUMBER

In a 1936 game against the Chicago Bears, Detroit Lions coach Potsy Clark kept yelling at his quarterback Dutch Clark to run play No. 27.

But Dutch paid no attention to the coach even though Potsy kept screaming, "Call number 27!"

Finally Bears defensive back Carl Brumbaugh shouted to Dutch across the line of scrimmage, "For heaven's sake, Dutch, why don't you call number 27 before Potsy blows up!"

Against his better judgment, Dutch ran the play and the Lions lost five yards. As the teams lined up again, Brumbaugh yelled over to the Detroit bench, "Hey, Potsy, what do you want Dutch to do now?"

The chagrined coach replied, "Tell him to tell me to keep my big mouth shut."

PRICE FIXING

Washington State Cougars coach Mike Price psyched up his team in the wackiest ways in 1989.

Before the Arizona State game, he showed up looking like a goofy version of ASU's mascot, Sparky the Sun Devil (see photo). Clad in hot pink tights, horns, and a flowing black cape, the zany coach brandished a pitchfork as he urged his Cougars to beat the hell out of the Sun Devils. But WSU lost 44–39.

In preparation for an upcoming game against Southern Cal, Price hired an actor to portray the USC Trojan and gallop onto the WSU practice field astride a white horse. As his surprised team watched, Price whipped out a starter's pistol loaded with blanks and blazed away at the interloper who slumped in the saddle and rode away "mortally" wounded. But WSU lost 18–17.

Price's get-up gags finally worked after he disguised himself as a duck hunter before the game against the Oregon Ducks. Price, decked out in a hunting outfit and waders, stalked the gridiron while toting a shotgun and a bagful of dead ducks. WSU won 51–38.

GLOOMY GIL DOBIE

Coach ■ North Dakota State–Washington–Navy–Cornell– Boston College ■ 1906–38

They called him Mr. Gloom, the Sad Scot, the Apostle of Grief, the Prince of Pessimism. But mostly they called him Gloomy Gil—for good reason.

No head football coach was more of a killjoy than Gloomy Gil Dobie. He was an incurable spoilsport who found the bad in everything no matter how good things really were.

Once when a sportswriter reminded Dobie that his team had three of the fastest running backs in the country, the joyless coach glumly replied, "Sure, I know that. But this means they only get to the tacklers all the sooner."

Another time, when his team marched off the field with a 49–0 triumph, an enthusiastic alumnus thumped him on the back and said, "Now you must be happy." Dobie's face turned sour and he answered, "Happy? Why? What's going to happen to us next week?"

Before every game, Gloomy Gil moaned that his team was outmanned; that the situation was hopeless; and that his boys didn't stand a chance. He cornered the market on crying towels, and his were soaked every Saturday afternoon whether his team won or lost.

Mostly his boys won. In his 33 years of coaching, Dobie's teams compiled a remarkable 180–45–15 record for an impressive .780 winning percentage. Fourteen of his squads were undefeated.

From 1908 through 1916, his University of Washington team never lost, winning 58 games and tying three. But you'd never know it by the way the calamity howler talked.

Wee Coyle, who quarterbacked the Huskies from 1908 through 1911, recalled, "Before every game, Dobie would tell me, 'Kid, listen to me. We're going to get licked.' He'd say the opponents were 'great, big monsters and we haven't got a prayer, but we'll do the best we can.' We couldn't beat anybody it seemed."

Dobie couldn't dish out praise any more than he could throw a football the length of the field.

In 1920, his Cornell team was leading Colgate by a touchdown when a Colgate back broke loose in the final seconds of the first half. Cornell's sophomore defensive end Dave Munns was the last man between him and the goal. Munns grabbed his man by the wrist and swung him around three times before they both fell to the turf. The gun sounded and Munns strode joyously into the locker room only to be stopped by Dobie. "I suppose you're proud of that tackle," said the taciturn coach. "If his arm had come off, they would've had six points."

Heroes could do no right. When Dobie was coaching at Boston College, pint-sized halfback Til Ferdenzi caught a pass in the end zone late in the game to beat North Carolina State 7–3.

"I was pretty proud and happy, especially when I was awarded the game ball," Ferdenzi recalled. "But then Dobie leaped in front of me, yanked the ball out of my arms, and shouted, 'No little peasant is going to improve on my plays and get away with it!' Gil was raging because I made the catch in the middle of the end zone and not in the corner, where I should have been, according to the diagram. The reason I wasn't there was because the primary area was all cluttered up. Anyway, he gave me the football back a week later and muttered something about my having made a good play. The old bastard made me sweat a full week, though."

Gloomy Gil seemed to take a sadistic delight in disparaging the abilities of his players. For example, in 1921, after his Cornell team had walloped Dartmouth 59–7, fans were shocked to see the Big Red in a practice scrimmage immediately after the game. When asked why,

Dobie answered sullenly, "Those bums didn't expect to get away with *that* performance, did they?"

At the end of the 1923 season, when Cornell had whipped Penn 14–7 to wrap up its third straight undefeated season, Dobie was congratulated on another Ivy League championship. The cynical coach snapped back, "If this is a championship team, then the human race must be degenerating!"

That's how cheerful he was when his teams were *winning*. His misery and rage were boundless when they were losing.

In 1935, after Princeton clobbered Cornell 54–0, Dobie told his players that they should publicly absolve him of the blame. "After all," he pointed out, "I'm just the coach."

The day before the Big Red was drubbed 41–6 at Dartmouth, Dobie, sensing impending disaster, escorted his players on a tour around the football field. Pointing to the 40-yard line, he said sarcastically, "You kick off here." Then he walked them over to their bench and told the players in a condescending voice, "This is where you sit when you're not playing." Finally, he marched them down to the 10-yard line and said, "And here is where you'll be all afternoon with your backs to the wall."

Over the years, his hopeless wailing began wearing thin. Some sportswriters believed that Dobie predicted the worst so that he could make himself appear to be something of a miracle man if his team happened to win. If his boys lost, that was only what should have been expected.

Explaining why he was always so glum, Gloomy Gil said, "A football coach can only wind up two ways—dead or a failure."

BUT IT'S NOT IN THE PLAYBOOK

Before Lionel Taylor became a star receiver for the Denver Broncos, he played briefly with the Chicago Bears.

Unfortunately, he seldom got the chance to play for Coach George Halas.

Finally, late in the fourth quarter of a 1960 preseason game against the Pittsburgh Steelers, Halas called down the bench for Taylor. The rookie thought he'd finally get to show the old man how good a pass catcher he was.

"What do you want me to do, Coach?" Taylor asked eagerly.

"We've run out of timeouts," Halas replied. "Go in and get hurt."

CAMPUS CAPERS

Rivalries are like loud belches—they bring out the worst in people. The annual clashes between college rivals have grown so intense they have turned into old-fashioned, jaw-to-jaw, knuckles-down gut checks—for the fans! Raiders, pranksters, and saboteurs have invaded each other's campuses in a ridiculous show of one-upmanship. Even the players get caught up in the annual madness. For "The Wildest Rivalries in Football," The Football Hall of SHAME inducts the following:

ARMY-NAVY

1890–Present

Following the 1893 Army-Navy game, a general and an admiral blasted away at each other in the only duel ever touched off by a football game.

Fortunately, the duelists were such lousy shots that they both missed. But the silly shootout so upset President Grover Cleveland that he ordered Army and Navy to stop playing each other to protect the lives of America's top military leaders. The ban lasted six years.

When the teams met in the 1893 clash, both had lost four games and were grimly determined to wrap up the season with a victory. And while the Army-Navy rivalry was only three years old, the top brass already viewed the game as a life-and-death struggle over bragging rights for the entire U.S. military establishment.

The Army-Navy struggle quickly deteriorated into a nasty slugfest and the rowdyism spread to the spectators who were allowed to stand along the sidelines. As the game reached its brawling climax with "brave old Army" going down to a 6–4 defeat, a brigadier general

punched a fancily dressed rear admiral who had been giving Army hell all day.

With his honor more bruised than his nose, the admiral challenged the general to a duel. They later met in secret at Washington's Army and Navy Club and blazed away at each other from 20 paces—and missed. But the uproar over the duel prompted President Cleveland to cancel future Army-Navy games. Six years later, in 1899, a new administration rescinded the order and the football series resumed.

Nearly a century after it started, the rivalry between the Cadets and the Middies remains just as exuberant—but not as deadly—as in the days of the duelists. Instead of weapons at dawn, the two schools now engage in an endless round of sophomoric pranks intended to make the other look as foolish as possible. Public embarrassment has become as much a part of the spectacle as the game itself.

Beneath the pomp and the pageantry of the crisp blue and gray units marching smartly into the stadium before each game lie carefully concealed water balloons and jars of Limburger cheese. They're used to bomb or smear the opposition at appropriate times. More than once, the Cadets or the Middies have arrived in freshly pressed uniforms to find their seats even more freshly painted.

Many of the pregame escapades revolve around the Navy's goat, Billy, and the Army's mule mascots, Mr. Jackson and Poncho—which have all become endangered species in the week preceding the game. Billy Goat especially has been the main butt of Army's barnyard humor over the years.

In 1953, a raiding party from West Point sneaked into the Naval Academy and kidnapped Billy Goat XV. The hostage was shoved into the rear seat of a convertible and hustled back to West Point. But enroute, Billy ate the upholstery, kicked out the rear windows, and punched a hole in the roof. After the goat-napping, an ad appeared in *The New York Times* that read, "Hey, Navy! Do you know where your 'kid' is today?"

Billy (shown in photo with the Army mascot) was paraded through the cadet's mess hall as the "guest of honor" at a pregame pep rally. While Army pondered an impromptu mutton barbecue and Navy waited for a ransom note, the brass in the Pentagon stepped in and ordered Billy returned to Annapolis.

West Point's adjutant, Lt. Col. George W. McIntyre, led a party of five that escorted Billy back to Annapolis. "We stood all we could of that goat," said McIntyre. "He just added to the smog problem up here."

A huge rally was under way at Navy's Bancroft Hall when the Army escort party arrived. The West Pointers were surrounded by a mob of Middies chanting, "We want the Colonel!" McIntyre was pushed before the assembly and forced to apologize for Army's role in the kidnapping. "I am the adjutant of the Corps of Cadets," said McIntyre, "and for the past seven hours I've been aide to a goat. And right now, I feel like a bit of an ass speaking at a Navy rally."

Billy Goat has been the target of Army kidnappers several times during the century-old rivalry. And each attempt required that Navy enact a measure of revenge—such as the time the Middies barricaded themselves in the West Point chapel, played "Anchors Aweigh" on the organ, and piped it over the loudspeakers until they were finally driven out by an Army counterattack.

During ceremonies preceding the 1946 game, both mascots made bizarre entrances designed to mock the opposition.

First, a group clad in Army gray wheeled a huge wooden replica of the Army mule onto the field. The Corps of Cadets rose to its feet and cheered the surprise appearance of their powerful symbol as it passed before the Army cheering section.

But the structure was nothing more than a modern version of the Trojan horse. When it reached Navy's side of the field, a door sprang open and out charged a snorting, defiant Billy X, as the Navy cheerleaders peeled off their fake Army costumes to the delight of the Midshipmen.

But Navy didn't have long to gloat. Minutes later, the replicas of a tank and a battleship moved out and circled the field. The tank stopped in front of the Cadets while the battleship halted across the field.

At a signal, the tank burst open and Poncho and Mr. Jackson galloped out. Then the tank's gun swung around and fired a salvo at the wooden battleship across the field. The symbol of the Navy collapsed in a dense cloud of smoke as the "sailors" on board abandoned ship.

In 1952, a Navy destroyer-escort, the *USS DeLong,* was anchored at West Point's South Dock the week before the game. Early one evening, the ship's watch was distracted by a couple of skimpy-skirted blondes who strolled onto the pier. The ogling sailors lost all interest in their duties when the sexpots produced drinks and snacks and the hint of more treats to come.

While Navy's attention was diverted, Army was running a flanker movement. Cadets manning a sailboat crept up to the opposite side of the ship and in big, black letters painted "Go Army, Beat Navy" on the vessel.

As soon as the job was finished, the Cadets gave a signal and the girls from Army's welcome wagon suddenly gathered up their goodies and disappeared into the night.

When the desecration was discovered the next morning, a pair of photographers from West Point's yearbook, *The Howitzer,* just happened to be rowing by and recorded Navy's humiliation. Sailors from the *DeLong* launched a pursuit craft and seized the camera-carrying Cadets in true pirate fashion. Not only was their film confiscated, but the Cadets were placed on a scaffold, lowered over the side, and not allowed to leave until the offending slogan had been scraped off the ship.

Masquerading as the opposition in order to shame one side or the other has always been a big part of the Army-Navy rivalry.

For example, Navy once had a human mascot, a character called Super Straight, who was sort of a poor man's Superman complete with cape and fighter pilot's helmet. Before one game in the mid-1970s, Super Straight filched a Cadet uniform and marched with the Corps during their dramatic entrance into the stadium. Once the formation reached the middle of the field, the impostor stripped off the hated Army gray. He then cavorted about in his Navy blue and gold Super Straight costume, taunting the Cadets, who were forced to remain at attention and submit to the character's raucous insults.

That incident was captured live on network television and inspired a summit conference between the academies aimed at reducing the pranks—and the national embarrassment. But the hijinks still continue.

CLEMSON–SOUTH CAROLINA

1896–Present

The fierce rivalry between the Clemson Tigers and South Carolina Gamecocks has besmirched the mascots and traditions of both schools.

One year, Clemson students started a mini-riot when they arrived at the game bearing a huge platter of fried chicken and oversized knives and forks. South Carolina supporters were outraged by this mocking of their gamecock mascot and invaded the Tiger cheering section. Police separated the two sides, but the Clemson fried chicken was trampled underfoot in the melee.

Later, the Gamecocks got even for the mockery. They beat Clemson, then set fire to a huge handmade Tiger and danced around the bonfire while the South Carolina band played "Taps."

A fight also broke out after South Carolina students pulled off their most elaborate prank shortly before the 1961 game. They impersonated the Tigers football team.

Members of the Sigma Nu fraternity, in collusion with South Carolina Coach Marvin Bass, collected a full set of uniforms that matched the Clemson colors. A heavyset fraternity brother was chosen to portray the Tigers' hefty coach Frank Howard. The group of bogus players practiced in secret for a month prior to the game to make their ruse look as realistic as possible. Bass even provided a locker room at the stadium where the plotters suited up.

While the real Clemson team was still getting dressed, the fake Tigers trotted onto the field for pregame warmups. Ronald Leitch, who played the role of Howard, wore an old brown suit and fedora and stuck wads of bubblegum in his cheeks to give him the ample Howard look.

The hoax was so successfully executed that as soon as the impostors ran out of the visitors' tunnel, the Clemson band struck up "Tiger Rag," the school fight song, and hundreds of cheering Clemson rooters rose to their feet.

The charade might have continued until the real Clemson team emerged. But the imitation Tigers began to deliberately botch their practice drills. Kickers missed the ball, receivers dropped passes, and blockers flopped flat on their faces. Even then, the Clemson crowd still wasn't sure it had been bamboozled until Chubby Checker's "Peppermint Twist" blared from the public address system and the masqueraders began to shimmy and shake.

A gang of furious Clemson boosters stormed the field in pursuit of the impostors. The pushing and shoving that followed resulted in little more than bruised egos.

However, the brief skirmish would have turned into all-out war if the South Carolina pranksters had been able to finish the sham as scheduled. A bony, sickly old milk cow had been hidden beneath the stands. The plan was to parade it out at halftime and introduce the cow as Clemson's homecoming queen. But in all the excitement, the old Bossy had a heart attack and dropped dead.

Pregame ribbing of the other team has become a tradition. Frank "Gator" Farr, a Clemson alumnus, made an annual pilgrimage from his home in Florida to conduct a mock funeral of a stuffed chicken the night before the big game. An honor guard escorted a coffin bearing a huge chicken. Then for half an hour, Gator Farr, who was all decked out in top hat and tails, "preached" over the Gamecock's remains, taking as his text the ladies' ready-to-wear section from the Sears, Roebuck catalog. The tongue-in-cheek ceremonies concluded with a snake dance through town and a bonfire.

In 1925, a South Carolina fan tried to upstage the Clemson cadets who were performing their snappy drill routines at halftime. He fell in behind the unit and imitated the marchers using a cane as a rifle. All went well, with the crowd applauding his antics, until the corps did a sudden about face. The interloper was trampled underfoot and left sprawled in the dust.

The frenzied rivalry boiled over in 1946 as thousands of fans— including many who had unwittingly bought tickets from a counterfeiter—tore down the walls to see the game. Unrecognized, Clemson coach Frank Howard and his team had to battle their way through the mob and convince stadium guards to let them in. Even then, Howard was almost locked out until he angrily announced that unless he was allowed inside there wouldn't be any game at all.

By game time, every seat was taken, while the angry crowd outside the stadium had swelled to nearly 10,000. They all held tickets they claimed were legitimate. As the Tigers and Gamecocks lined up for the kickoff, two large wooden gates at each end of the stadium gave way under the crush and a human wave of gate crashers poured onto the field.

Since there was no room for them in the stands, the thousands of unexpected rooters ringed the sidelines five and six deep. Several times, officials had to stop play to clear away the overwrought spectators and make room for the players. Fans mingled with team members, offered them slugs from smuggled flasks, and kibitzed with both coaches on how the game should be played.

"It was impossible to do any coaching," recalled Howard. "I'd look around to yell for a substitute and there would be 50 people between me and my bench. Most of the people on the ground level just sat around talking to old friends because they couldn't see a thing out on the field. Hell, I even had hawkers come up to me and try to sell me their wares right during the game."

Even the powerful politicians, who were usually given the best seats on the 50-yard line, saw little of the game. Secretary of State James H. Byrnes was among the dignitaries. After his box seat was overrun, Byrnes spent most of the game on his hands and knees peeking between the legs of players and coaches on the South Carolina sideline to see the action on the field.

At halftime, Governor-elect Strom Thurmond and his party were being escorted from the Clemson stands to the South Carolina side of the field. As they walked across the gridiron, a wild squawking erupted from one end zone. Two Clemson students dashed out onto the field strewing feathers in their wake. They had seized South Carolina's gamecock mascot and were plucking the bird as they ran. The pair halted near the group of politicians and wrung the bird's neck until it was dead in full view of thousands of infuriated South Carolina fans.

One account claimed the late chicken was really a Rhode Island Red that had been bootlegged into the stadium for the occasion. The bird's ancestry didn't matter. Clemson had made its point and South Carolina rooters charged out to avenge the insult. The executioners escaped into police custody.

AIRING IT OUT

In 1946, just days before the Yale Bulldogs–Princeton Tigers game, Yale commandos stormed Princeton's radio station, WPRU, and took control of its programming for a few hours. The pirated broadcast opened with the Yale fight song and then aired a series of insults and innuendoes questioning the masculinity of the Tigers' football team.

Princeton students were outraged when they tuned to their campus radio station and heard nothing but anti-Tigers and pro-Bulldogs propaganda.

By the time the furious Princeton students reclaimed the station, the commandos had already disappeared, leaving behind a pre-recorded tape still blaring out the slanderous slurs.

The Bulldogs' "air raid" was in retaliation for an early-morning Princeton foray onto the Yale campus. Tigers fans had sneaked into the stadium, where the game was going to be played, and burned a huge "P" in the middle of the football field.

SOUTHERN CAL–UCLA

1929–Present

Ever since their rivalry began, the University of Southern California and the University of California at Los Angeles have expressed their loathing for each other with campus raids, manure bombs, and sabotaged pep rallies.

The USC–UCLA rivalry is one made in Hollywood heaven—blue-collar, working-class UCLA versus snobbish, affluent USC for intra-city bragging rights. The public school against the private school. To top it off, both teams are PAC-10 foes and perennial national powerhouses. The outcome of the USC–UCLA game often determines which of the rivals appears in postseason bowl games and has even decided national championships.

"The game is not a matter of life and death," said former UCLA coach Red Sanders. "It's more important than that."

For years, Bruin students from UCLA delighted in raiding the USC campus before the game. They would find Traveler—USC's beloved white horse that carries the Trojan warrior into the stadium on game day—and paint him with a coat of Bruin blue. "Tommy Trojan," a statue on campus that symbolizes USC athletics, was the next favorite target for a new blue paint job (see photo). Once, pranksters broke off the Trojan's sword and welded it to his back.

By 1958, UCLA students wanted something that more accurately reflected the depths of their feelings toward the despised Trojans.

So the Bruins rented a helicopter, collected several bags of manure from a nearby riding stable, and headed for the USC campus. With the chopper hovering over Southern Cal's revered statue of Tommy Trojan, the fertilizing crew opened the bags and began dumping the droppings on top of Tommy. But the odorous mess, whipped up by the copter's whirling blades, blew right back in their faces!

For years afterward, Tommy Trojan spent the week before the big game wrapped like a mummy in something resembling a giant Baggie to stymie any paintbrush-wielding, doo-doo-dropping Bruins.

The aborted manure bombing run was itself a payback for a devious piece of chicanery inflicted on UCLA. Trojan schemers had invaded the office of the *Daily Bruin* (UCLA's student newspaper) and replaced stories, photos, and captions with those written by USC students. The bogus edition was distributed as the real thing. Shocked UCLA students read their quarterback saying, "I'd feel much better about our chances against those terrific Trojans if we had a couple of players who understood the game." And the UCLA coach viewed the upcoming USC game with despair. "I don't see any hope for our team," read his phony quote.

A tradition of pranks has a long and checkered past. Mice painted with USC initials were released in the UCLA library. UCLA smoke bombs went off under Southern Cal's rooting section. A huge stack of wood for a bonfire at a USC pep rally was prematurely torched by a couple of Bruins. In 1975, USC students sent out a notice on purloined UCLA stationery and successfully canceled a giant pep rally that had been planned for weeks by Bruin supporters.

USC students also once tapped into the UCLA classrooms' public address system. All day long, the Southern Cal fight song blared out while the Bruins were forced to endure verse after verse of "Fight on for Old SC."

Insulting buttons, banners, and bumper stickers appear each year to fuel the already heated rivalry. Some USC favorites have been: "I Used to Go to UCLA Until My Father Got a Job"; "*U* Clowns *Lost* Again"; "My Maid Went to UCLA"; and "U$C–U¢LA—You Get What You Pay For." Over at UCLA the buttons have read: "SUC";

"University of Social Climbers"; "University of Spoiled Children"; "USC—The Best Football Team Money Can Buy"; and "Trojans Always Break."

The mutual dislike really began in the 1939 game when a group of Bruins brought an old Southern Pacific locomotive bell and started ringing the 295-pound monster after every UCLA touchdown. The thunderous clang irritated the Trojans to no end and quickly became a symbol for all they detested about the Bruins.

So the Trojans plotted to steal the bell when UCLA played Washington in the first game of the 1941 season. Six members of a USC fraternity swallowed their pride and disguised themselves as Bruin rooters. After the game, they helped load what had now become known as the Victory Bell into a truck for the trip back to UCLA's Westwood campus. But while the Bruin bell ringers were distracted, the conspirators stole the truck and drove off with the bell.

For a year, thieves moved the bell from one hiding place to another, including a haystack at Santa Ana. Probes by UCLA raiders and even threats by L.A. police failed to produce the bell. Finally, the presidents of both student bodies met in a truce summit. USC agreed to return the Victory Bell on the condition that it become a permanent game trophy.

UCLA's 13–6 win in 1946 touched off a campus-to-campus melee when carloads of gloating Bruins invaded USC's turf.

Earlier, four Trojans had been assigned to take the bell across town and hand it over to the winners. Unfortunately, they picked a bad time to show up. More than 5,000 UCLA students had blocked the Westwood streets in celebration and the arrival of the Victory Bell sent them into a frenzy.

A caravan of honking, shouting, banner-waving Bruins then chased the outnumbered Trojans back across town to rub a little salt in USC's wounds. But the winners got more than they bargained for from the unhappy losers, who poured from dorms and classrooms and captured 10 carloads of UCLA supporters.

The cars were stripped of wiring, spark plugs, hoods, fenders, seats, and tires, and then smeared with paint. A UCLA jeep was pushed into a pond. USC students shaved the heads of the male captives, painted "SC" on their scalps, and forced them to scrub Tommy Trojan which—as usual—had been daubed with blue paint. Several Bruin coeds were dunked in a fountain before they were sent home in disgrace.

It was also the year that George Tirebiter arrived at USC. George was a mongrel hound who got his name because he liked to bite car tires—while they were still moving. The bizarre pooch was given an old football helmet to wear and, with the backing of the student newspaper, became the school's unofficial mascot.

George Tirebiter rode to the UCLA games in the front seat of a shiny convertible, disembarked before a cheering Trojan rooting section, and spent the afternoon barking at Bruins.

Bruin fans hated that dog and he hated anything wearing UCLA's blue and gold. In 1947, some Bruins snatched Tirebiter and shaved "U-C-L-A" in his fur before releasing the mutt on the USC campus. But to the chagrin of the UCLA rooters, Tirebiter appeared at the game draped in a Trojan blanket to hide the disgraceful slogan.

Tirebiter died in 1950 when he bit a tire—and forgot to let go. USC mourned. UCLA celebrated.

AUBURN GREASERS

Nov. 7, 1896

The rivalry between Georgia Tech and Auburn has sizzled ever since the Auburn students literally railroaded the Tech football team.

The scheming students lathered the railroad tracks with slimy pig grease and then stood watching as the arriving Georgia Tech train skidded right through town. The train wasn't able to stop until it was almost five miles down the line. Because the tracks were too slick for the engine to gain traction to back up, the disgruntled Tech players had to disembark. Then they had to lug their own equipment all the way back to the Auburn field.

There, the Yellow Jackets were so wiped out by the unscheduled trek that they were whomped by Auburn 45–0.

The prank unfolded during the first Wreck Tech Pajama Parade in 1896. Ever since, the parade has been a hallowed pregame tradition at Auburn. Each year, students clad in pajamas have marched to the home stadium chanting, "Wreck Tech, wreck Tech, wreck the hell out of Georgia Tech!"

The first parade was supposed to end at the football field. Instead, it ended early in the morning at the train station where the Auburn fans decided to ignite a rivalry that has flamed for nearly a century.

Although he never owned up to it, Auburn coach John Heisman allegedly instigated the prank to distract the opposition and give his Tigers the edge in the game.

Ironically, the chief prankster was the very same coach who eventually had a trophy named after him—a trophy symbolizing the best in college football.

"The Auburn football team's upperclassmen ordered the freshmen to start laying in a supply of pig grease several days before the game," said David Housel, Auburn sports information director. "Since it was the first home game, the team wanted to do something to really make the event memorable."

Adding to the anticipation was the fact that Auburn and Georgia Tech were both engineering schools at the time and a fierce professional jealousy existed long before the two schools met on the gridiron.

Early on the morning of the big game, the freshmen, still clad in their pajamas, retrieved the stash of pig grease they had collected from farms and slaughterhouses in the area, and greased several hundred feet of rails with the smelly goo.

Then students lined both sides of the tracks as the Tech Special chugged into town from the east—and they waved and cheered as the train slid out of town to the west.

The fans were still at the station hours later when the weary Tech football team came trudging back along the greased tracks. That afternoon, Tech faced another greasing on the football field.

The prank irritated the Yellow Jackets so much that they refused to return to Auburn until they were guaranteed that no more pranks awaited them. Auburn agreed, but when Georgia Tech arrived for a game two years later, a contingent of greaseless, pajama-clad Auburn students greeted them at the station just to remind the Yellow Jackets of their 45–0 drubbing.

PENALTY PANDEMONIUM

Football is like a great literary work—Crime and Punishment. With the way some players try to get away with murder during games, you'd swear that they lettered at Attica. But, like chronic felons, they usually get caught red-handed. Referees have thrown enough flags at these offenders to cover the gridiron. For "The Most Inglorious Infractions Ever Committed," The Football Hall of SHAME inducts the following:

COLORADO STATE RAMS

Oct. 5, 1974

The Colorado State Rams celebrated too long, too loud—and too soon.

They were flagged for their overexuberance and it wound up costing them a last-second victory.

Colorado State was losing to the Brigham Young University Cougars 33–27 with just six seconds left to play. Although BYU was deep in its own territory, all Cougar quarterback Gary Sheide had to do was fall on the ball to guarantee a victory.

Rams fans were filing out of Hughes Stadium in Ft. Collins, Colorado, after what looked like a disappointing end to a thrilling emotional roller coaster ride.

But when Sheide set up for what should have been the final play of the game, the roller coaster suddenly roared to life again. Incredibly, he fumbled and a Colorado State defender recovered the ball with three seconds left in the game.

As time ran out, Rams quarterback Mark Driscoll hit flanker Willie Miller in the corner of the end zone to knot the score at 33-all. That touched off pandemonium on the sidelines and in the stands.

Players, coaches, and students swarmed into the end zone and mobbed Miller. The bedlam continued for several minutes while officials frantically tried to shoo the wild celebrants off the field for the extra point try.

Finally, the penalty flag flew. The Rams were called for unsportsmanlike conduct—or, as an official put it, "interference with orderly game administration." Since the game was over, the penalty was tacked on when Colorado State lined up for the PAT. What should have been an easy kick to win the game turned out to be a tough 35-yard boot.

Clark Kemble kicked what he thought was the winning point. At least, he said later, "It looked close to being good."

Back judge Jack Combs knew better. He signaled the kick was wide. But referee Jack Moyers wigwagged a bunch of signals—first good, then wide, then what looked like good again.

The scoreboard flashed the good news: Colorado State Rams 34, Visitors 33. The jubilant Rams headed for the locker room and the celebration began in earnest.

Shouting, cheering, and hugging each other, the boisterous players hoisted Willie Miller onto their shoulders and paraded him around the locker room in honor of his touchdown reception. Coach Sark Arslanian told his delirious team: "This is the sweetest victory of my career! Words can't describe how I feel!"

But the roller coaster ride had one more giant dip to go. John Adams, the supervisor of the Western Athletic Conference officials, pushed his way into the tumultuous locker room and, over the din, announced that Colorado State had not won after all.

Referee Moyers' hands-in-the-air signal had not indicated the extra point try was good. WAC rules called for the official to hold the ball over his head to signal the end of the game. When Moyers couldn't find the ball in the turmoil, he had held up just his hands instead. Actually, the kick was wide and the game ended in a 33–33 tie.

FINGER FOOD

In a 1960 game against the Green Bay Packers, Los Angeles Rams linebacker Les Richter made a crushing tackle on fullback Jimmy Taylor.

Apparently, Taylor had missed lunch that day because in the pileup, he started to snack on Richter's finger. Les then showed his bitten finger to the ref and demanded that Green Bay be flagged for a 15-yard penalty.

The ref looked at the teeth marks on Richter's finger and said, "It didn't draw blood yet. No penalty."

Richter turned to Taylor and said, "Next time, bite it clean off. We need the yardage."

WALT SWEENEY

Defensive End ■ Syracuse Orangemen ■ Nov. 18, 1961

Because of the overzealousness of Syracuse defensive end Walt Sweeney, the Orangemen had to return to the field after time had expired to lose a game they already had won.

Sweeney was flagged for unnecessary roughness on the final play of the game for plowing into both the Notre Dame kicker and holder on a failed field goal attempt. The stunning penalty gave the Fighting Irish another field goal try. This time, they didn't miss and Notre Dame won in a storybook 17–15 victory.

The devastating reversal followed one of the hardest-fought games ever played in South Bend. Syracuse held tenaciously to a 15–14 lead when the Fighting Irish launched a last-ditch drive from their own 30-yard line with only 17 seconds left to play.

A 21-yard run and a 10-yard pass put the ball on the Orangemen's 39-yard line with only three seconds left in the game. If Notre Dame was to pull it out, victory would have to come from the toe of kicker Joe Perkowski.

But not if Sweeney could help it. With everything on the line, he was determined to block the kick.

With 50,000 fans screaming themselves hoarse, Perkowski attempted the field goal from the 46-yard line. To the joy of the Orangemen, the kick was far short and way to the right.

The jubilant Syracuse players dashed off the field in triumph as the Notre Dame faithful watched in stunned silence.

But in all the commotion, few noticed the penalty flag fluttering to the ground or referee Gus Skibbie frantically waving his arms. Syracuse's hard-won celebration was suddenly cut short as Skibbie pointed to Sweeney and called a penalty against him for unnecessary roughness.

In his zeal to block the kick, Sweeney had slammed not only into holder George Sefcik but into kicker Perkowski as well. "He tore so savagely into the kicker, slow-motion movies of the play horrified viewers," wrote one sportswriter.

As a result, officials called both teams back onto the field to replay the down even though there was no time left on the clock. The 15-yard penalty moved the ball to the Syracuse 24-yard line. Handed a second chance, and with the Syracuse defenders in a daze over the unbelievable turnaround, Perkowski booted the clutch field goal through the uprights for an incredible 17–15 Notre Dame victory.

Dejected Syracuse coach Floyd Schwartzwalder could only shake his head over the crushing defeat. "It's one of those things you believe didn't happen," he muttered.

MOCO MERCER

Coach ■ Dubuque Spartans ■ Oct. 11, 1952

In one of the most bizarre penalties ever assessed in a college football game, the Dubuque Spartans lost 1–0 on a forfeit—thanks to their coach's foul mouth.

With most of the fourth quarter still to go and his team trailing by a touchdown, Coach Moco Mercer turned the air blue with his profane protests over a trick play by Iowa Wesleyan. As the outburst continued, referee Fran DeReus ran out of patience and levied the ultimate penalty. He picked up the ball and declared a rare forfeit, giving Wesleyan the victory.

It happened during the Wesleyan Tigers' homecoming at Mt. Pleasant, Iowa, in 1952. With about 12 minutes left in the fourth quarter and trailing 7–0, Dubuque started a drive.

At his own 21-yard line, quarterback Cantrill Gulliford faded back to pass, but he was hit and fumbled. A Tiger recovered the ball and ran it in for an apparent score.

The referee's TD signal brought Coach Mercer, trailed by his coaching staff, storming onto the field to argue that the ball had hit the ground on the 11-yard line and should have been downed at that point. Wesleyan coach E. R. Jarvis and his assistants rushed out to voice their own opinions. Since the clock was stopped during an official timeout, the debate raged for several minutes.

Finally, DeReus agreed with Mercer. The touchdown call was reversed and the ball was brought back to the 11-yard line in Wesleyan's possession. Dubuque then called a timeout to tend to an injured player.

In the midst of all the jawboning, Tigers halfback Bob Bogdonas wandered near the Wesleyan bench and lost himself in the crowd of Tigers standing on the sideline. By the time play resumed, the Spartans didn't notice that Bogdonas was only a yard in from the sideline but on the line of scrimmage.

On the play, quarterback Dick Schmitt flipped a quick pass to the unnoticed Bogdonas who then ran all the way to the 1-yard line before being stopped. When the dust had cleared, Mercer was back out on the field and in DeReus's face bellowing that this particular sleeper play was against the rules.

A sleeper play was illegal following an official timeout, he argued. But DeReus pointed out that a Dubuque timeout had followed the official timeout and that made the play legal.

Mercer wasn't buying it. The language he used to make his point was seldom heard around the reserved Wesleyan campus. Finally, his ears burning, DeReus gave Mercer two minutes to stop the profanity and get off the field or he'd start marking off penalties against the Spartans.

"He told me he didn't care if I moved the ball half the distance to the goal line all night long," DeReus recalled. "Only those weren't the words he used. I'd rather not repeat exactly what he said."

But the coach continued his loud cussing and fussing. After the shocked fans in the stands learned a few more dirty words that they'd never heard before, DeReus picked up the ball and marched off the field announcing to a suddenly speechless Moco Mercer: "The game is forfeited."

As supporters poured onto the field and the jubilant Tigers celebrated their weird victory, the Spartans surrounded their coach and bad-mouthed his foul mouth for losing the game.

One witness described the scene on the field as "something like downtown Detroit during rush hour. . . . A confusing time was had by all."

The bizarre outcome scrambled the statistics for both teams. Wesleyan had been scoring a healthy 33.5 points per game. But that average dropped to 24 due to the 1–0 forfeit victory. And Dubuque, with a record of 1–1 following the forfeit, still had outscored its opponents 13–1!

RICK ABERNATHY

Linebacker ▪ Kansas Jayhawks ▪ Jan. 1, 1969

Kansas linebacker Rick Abernathy caused the costliest and most infamous penalty in bowl-game history.

In the final seconds of the 1969 Orange Bowl, the Jayhawks had apparently stopped the Penn State Nittany Lions for a 14–13 victory. But Kansas was flagged for having 12 men on the field because Abernathy had failed to leave when his replacement was sent in. As a result, the Nittany Lions were given a second chance to run a play. They made the most of the reprieve and scored the winning points.

"I coached the only Kansas team ever to win the Big Eight Championship," said Pepper Rodgers, "and I have spent the rest of my life explaining how we lost the Orange Bowl with 12 men on the field." Here's how Kansas blew it:

The sixth-ranked Jayhawks were desperately hanging on to a 14–7 lead over the third-ranked and undefeated Nittany Lions, who had the ball on the 50-yard line with 1:16 left in the game. Penn State then completed a dramatic 47-yard pass, putting the ball on the 3-yard line.

Coach Rodgers immediately switched to a goal-line defense. He sent in two tackles to replace two linebackers—but only one linebacker came out. The other one, Rick Abernathy, was so intent on stopping the Nittany Lions that he didn't notice the substitutions. Besides, neither tackle had tapped him on the shoulder, which was the team signal to head for the bench.

"Everything was mass confusion at that point," recalled Abernathy. "Penn State was running a hurry-up offense. There was noise and tension. It was total pandemonium.

"I was so concerned about stopping them that I didn't think about what was going on. I do remember that it seemed a little crowded in our huddle."

The outnumbered Nittany Lions tried two running plays. But because nobody blocked Abernathy, who was now Kansas' extra player, he stopped fullback Tom Cherry for no gain both times. "Our coaches in the press box were going nuts," recalled Penn State coach Joe Paterno. "They knew something was wrong because every hole we tried was plugged. But nobody did any counting."

On third down, and with only 15 seconds left in the game, quarterback Chuck Burkhart bootlegged around left end and scored against a 12-man defense that had yet to be detected by the officials.

The Nittany Lions now trailed 14–13. But rather than go for the tie with a kick, Paterno boldly ordered a do-or-die two-point conversion attempt.

Burkhart rolled to his right and attempted to pass to halfback Bob Campbell. But the Kansas defense rose to the challenge and knocked the ball away.

The jubilant Jayhawks began dancing in the end zone, congratulating each other. But their festivities were premature. Official Foster Grose had counted one too many Jayhawks and had thrown his flag.

"What's the flag for?" Abernathy asked Grose.

"Too many men on the field," the ref replied.

"Oh, no! I shouldn't have been out there," moaned Abernathy, his head bowed in shame as he trudged back to the bench.

Given a second chance because of the stunning penalty, the Nittany Lions scored the winning two-point conversion when Campbell smashed into the end zone. Final score: Penn State 15, Kansas 14.

"I knew I was the twelfth man," recalled Abernathy. "I was crushed. I have never had a more hollow feeling in my life. Death in the family couldn't have been any worse. I was the oldest player on the team, a five-year man, which made it hurt even more.

"I tried to tell myself those things happen in football. But when I got into the dressing room, everything was so depressingly quiet. I knew my teammates had to think that if I hadn't been in there, we would've won. That's when I broke. I sat in my stall and cried my eyes out.

"It was days before I could sort things out in my mind. With the passing of time, I got over it—and now I can even laugh about my 'contribution' to Orange Bowl history."

There's a reason why it's called halftime. No matter what's happened during the game, half the time what goes on between the second and third quarters is much more memorable. And nuttier. Colleges love to present marching bands in routines so wild and tasteless they make rock videos seem like kiddie fare. For "The Most Ridiculous Halftime Performances," The Football Hall of SHAME inducts the following:

CALTECH HOAXERS

Jan. 1, 1961 and Jan. 1, 1984

Caltech students hoodwinked an entire nation and royally embarrassed the University of Washington by sabotaging the school's card section during the 1961 Rose Bowl.

And the hoax became such a classic in Caltech lore that the Techies struck again during the 1984 Rose Bowl in a slightly altered version of the prank updated for the computer age.

In both cases, the California Institute of Technology didn't play in the Rose Bowl. In fact, Caltech doesn't even have a football team. But what the Techies lacked in pigskin prowess, they more than made up for in knavery.

Weeks before the 1961 Rose Bowl game between Washington and Minnesota, a gang of 14 mischievous Caltech students set out to sabotage Washington's vaunted student card section. The card flashers were famous for creating colorful, animated designs and slogans in flowing script during the halftime of Huskies games.

The Techies learned that the 2,232-member Washington card section, its director, all the cards, and the top secret instructions for each

stunt would be housed in a dormitory on the Long Beach State campus.

One of the Caltech students, impersonating a reporter for a high school newspaper, interviewed the director and pumped him for details on how the cards were numbered and arranged to make the stunts work so spectacularly. The phony reporter also carefully cased the joint. He discovered that the lock on the door to the dorm could be easily picked.

The Caltech gang returned that night, picked the lock, and stole a single instruction sheet from a stack the director had hidden behind a table. A printer was waiting nearby and 2,232 duplicates were run off.

The next day, while the members of the card section were off on a trip to Disneyland, the Caltech gang again sneaked into the dorm and this time swiped the director's own secret master plan that outlined the numbering and color code for each of the 14 card stunts planned for the game. With that information in hand, the Techies spread their 2,232 bogus instruction sheets out and began altering them with their own directions for stunts 10, 11, and 12.

After 10 hours of feverish work, the job was done. The Techies returned the revised instructions to the Long Beach dorm on their third lock-picking foray. Then they sat back and waited for their elaborate hoax to unfold.

At halftime on New Year's Day, the Washington card section looked sharp and impressive at first. But the capacity crowd of 100,000, the millions of TV viewers, the hysterical band of Techies, and the Huskies director watched as Washington's pride and joy began to self-destruct with stunt number 10.

The cards were supposed to spell out "Washington," but as the script letters were flashed, the word "Caltech" appeared instead (see photo). That stupendous blemish in the otherwise flawless card exhibition immediately segued into even greater embarrassment for the visitors. The letters for the eleventh stunt had been reversed in the faked instructions so that "Huskies" was transformed into "Seiksuh."

For stunt number 12, the face of the Huskie, Washington's fierce mascot, was supposed to appear. Instead, the Huskie's ears and facial features had been rearranged so that he came out looking like a slightly demented beaver—the Caltech mascot!

The card-section director was so rattled by the audacious sabotage of his cherished stunts that he dumped the remaining two stunts. The fact that Washington won the game 17–7 over Minnesota took some of the sting out of the mortifying affair.

Twenty-three years later, UCLA and Illinois were victimized by a new generation of Caltech despoilers who disrupted the 1984 Rose Bowl with sophisticated computer software rather than crude cardboard cards.

With high technology now at their disposal, Caltech hackers comfortably cooked up their scheme from miles away and tapped into the Rose Bowl's scoreboard computer system.

In the fourth quarter, the huge scoreboard suddenly lit up with the evidence of their high-tech hijinks. Instead of showing UCLA ahead of Illinois 38–9, the scoreboard read "Caltech 38, MIT 9"!

WASHINGTON & LEE
HALFTIME SCRIMMAGE

Oct. 23, 1987

In one of the most bizarre scenes ever witnessed at halftime, the Washington & Lee Generals conducted a full-contact scrimmage—right in the middle of the University of the South's homecoming ceremonies!

When the second period ended, the host Tigers football team filed into the locker room with a comfortable 24–7 lead. The band struck up the school song. Students and alumni rose as homecoming Queen Marian McPherson and her regal court were escorted to the center of the field for the formal crowning ceremonies.

But suddenly the solemn moment was shattered by the clash of pads and angry shouts from Washington & Lee Coach Gary Fallon, who was at one end of the field exhorting his players to hit harder. Fallon had kept his Generals on the field at halftime because he was steaming mad that his team was being so badly beaten.

Meanwhile, the once-happy homecoming crowd in Sewanee, Tennessee, fell silent and the traditional halftime event ground to a halt. Appalled fans watched helplessly as the Generals stole the spotlight from the dismayed queen. She stood by in tears while the noisy scrimmage continued.

University of the South Alumni Association Director Yogi Anderson was among the outraged onlookers. "People were shocked," he recalled. "No one could believe it. Most of us thought that the coach

DRESS FOR SUCCESS?

Penn State wears about the plainest uniforms in college football. But maybe it's for the best. If the Nittany Lions followed tradition, they would be wearing the school's original uniform colors—pink and black!

Back in 1887, the first year Penn State fielded a team, the Lions wore the silly color combo of pink and black. They even had a ridiculous cheer: "Yah! Yah! Yah! Yah! Wish, Wack—Pink, Black!"

had gone crazy or must be some kind of idiot to be spoiling our homecoming like that."

Retired Tigers coach Horace Moore did a slow burn while Fallon ranted at his players, oblivious to the disruption he was causing. "It was the worst thing I had seen in all my years of football," Moore fumed.

But Fallon's attempt to fire up his team blew up in his face. On the first play of the practice scrimmage, linebacker Chris Jerussi went down with a serious knee injury and had to be helped off the field.

And on the very next play, starting center Rowan Taylor, caught in a pileup, suffered a compound fracture of his leg. A sullen bunch of Generals gathered around their coach on the sideline while an ambulance pulled onto the field and carted their injured teammate off to the hospital.

Fearful that he might wipe out his entire team before the second half started, Fallon called off the scrimmage. Only then did the Tigers supporters go on with their homecoming ceremonies, now much subdued.

It was left to the Tiger team to exact revenge for the insult. They stormed back onto the field and trounced the Generals 38–13.

"Our team was pretty unhappy over them ruining our homecoming," said University of the South Coach Bill Samko. "Our kids did a pretty good job of getting even."

HARVARD MARCHING BAND

Oct. 4, 1966

During its halftime show, the Harvard band formed a pair of mouse ears in front of the Boston University cheering section and then scornfully derided their Beantown neighbors with a rendition of the *Mickey Mouse Club* theme song.

But the snide insult backfired on Harvard. The BU Terriers heard the slur in their locker room. Fed up with being treated like some second-rate Mickey Mouse operation, BU came roaring back like Mighty Mouse in the second half and whipped the favored Harvard Crimson for the first time since the series began in 1884.

BU quarterback Peter Yetten, the team's fiery inspirational leader, was incensed when he heard the derisive "M-I-C-K-E-Y M-O-U-S-E" being played by the Harvard band.

"Harvard and BU both had 3–0 records at the time," recalled Yetten. "We both had good teams, but Harvard had always looked down on us as second-class citizens from across the Charles River.

"We were behind 10–7 at halftime and when we heard that Mickey Mouse music, there was a mutiny in the locker room. Everybody was upset, but I guess I was madder than the others. So I stood up and yelled at them, 'Are we going to take this crap anymore? Everybody thinks we're Mickey Mouse. But let's go out and show them what we really are!' "

Terriers captain Pat Hughes, who went on to play 10 years in the NFL, said that Harvard's ill-timed serenade riled him more than any halftime performance he had heard during his entire football career.

"The visitors' dressing room at Harvard was right underneath the stands and we could hear what was going on," said Hughes. "We had never beaten Harvard and there was never any love lost between the two schools, so it was pretty obvious that the band was dumping on us. That was the last straw. When they played that song, they lit a bomb under us that blew up in Harvard's face.

"We were tired of being looked upon as a Mickey Mouse team. *The Boston Globe* had the Harvard, Boston College, or Holy Cross games all over the front pages. You'd have to go back to the obituaries to find anything about Boston University. We committed ourselves early in the season to breaking that image."

After halftime was over, Yetten led his aroused Terrier teammates back to the field on a mission. BU successfully shut down Harvard's highly rated offense, holding the Crimson to only 100 yards in total offense.

In the final quarter, Yetten engineered a dramatic 50-yard drive. He capped it off with a touchdown toss to halfback Gary Capehart to beat the Crimson, who were nine-point favorites.

The 13–10 victory over BU's despised and haughty rival touched off a wild celebration that lasted long into the night.

As the festivities continued, members of the Terriers' football squad gathered on the banks of the Charles River for a ceremony Boston University had been waiting nearly a century to perform. En masse, they peed in the river and sent a message downstream to the Harvard Crimson.

STANFORD MARCHING BAND

1963–Present

The Stanford University band is the only college band ever banned by its own school for its hysterical halftime exhibitions that have included organized mooning and a group pee-in.

Band members have elevated mockery to an art form. When they take the field at halftime, nothing is sacred. Not religion. Not politics. Not even that great untouchable football legend Knute Rockne.

One of the band's performances in 1988 was based on the theme "The Other Temptations of Christ," an irreverent spoof that drew a bushel of hate mail. Some of those temptations included going through the express checkout line with more than 10 items and using something other than a No. 2 pencil on a standardized test.

Anyone else would have thought twice about making fun of Notre Dame on the Irish's home turf. But not the Stanford band. During halftime in South Bend in 1988, they shamelessly mocked every tradition Notre Dame has held sacred for generations.

STANFORD NEWS SERVICE

First the band formed a human eyeball and announced it was the "Fighting Iris." Next came the outline of a fish with the tag line "Win One for the Kipper." A whale became "The Humpback of Notre Dame." The halftime insults climaxed when the band slithered off the field in the form of a lizard, or "Newt Rockne."

The band wouldn't be caught dead simply marching as it forms its bizarre patterns. It saunters. It waddles. Sometimes it strolls backward or dashes pell mell from one spot to another. Most of the time it just boogies. But it never marches.

Since 1963, the band has had only one Sousa march in its repertoire. Most of its tunes come from the Grateful Dead, the Tubes, or the Talking Heads, which qualifies it as "the World's Largest Rock and Roll Band."

Two themes have dominated Stanford formations—sex and current events. In the 1970s, the band shocked fans with a show dedicated to the kidnapping of Patty Hearst. Shows featuring phallic symbols; those dedicated to sperm and ovum; and, more recently, to condoms are among the band's favorites.

But what outrages most alumni is the sly way the band manages to slip four-letter words and innuendoes into its field routines. For years, the band presented four-letter formations that were dreamed up by a committee called the Stanford Marching Unit Thinkers (SMUT for short).

Inspired by SMUT, the band has been known to form words which, depending on the eye of the beholder, could unscramble into something obscene. School officials were upset over one formation that started with letters that spelled out "ITSH." But while everyone was thinking of another word, the band reassembled into "THIS."

Another began as "NEUT" and was supposed to change to read "TUNE." But it was sabotaged by the treacherous trombone section who thought it would be cute to change the "E" into a "C" so that the final version spelled out a less-than-ambiguous "NCUT."

Officials have been furious over the band's habit of dropping its drawers and shooting the audience a communal moon to cap off a halftime performance.

It's a tradition that originated in the protest days of the late 1960s and peaked during a 1970 game against Arkansas when band members exposed themselves to the rest of America during a televised halftime spectacular.

For years, Berkeley students responded to the moon glow by pelting the band with oranges. Later, they switched to frozen oranges when their barrages of fresh fruit failed to deter the Stanford flashers.

The band, complained one indignant alumnus, "must be hidden from view because of repeated instances of exhibitionism and public urination."

In 1986, in a game against Southern Cal, some well-oiled band members took mooning a step further. As long as they had their pants down, they felt, it was a convenient time to water the stadium turf at the conclusion of the game. Band manager Todd Olson shrugged off the incident, blaming it on a few wasted trumpet players. "These guys were out there with their pants down around their ankles and their shorts on and the next thing you know they were pissing on the field," said Olson.

Nevertheless, an indignant Andy Geiger, Stanford's director of athletics, promptly banned the band from performing during the UCLA and Berkeley games. "I can't trust them," Geiger fumed. "They don't have a level of taste and values that represent this place."

At its first appearance following Geiger's banishment, the band, giving a reasonable impersonation of a real university band, smartly marched onto the field at halftime playing "When the Saints Go Marching In." Each member sprouted a tinfoil halo and marched behind a banner proclaiming: "Sanitized For Your Protection."

The band, at times, has even angered its own football team. Once, before Stanford played at Oklahoma in 1984, band members sent a message to the Sooners describing the Oklahoma fans as "psychotic and frothing at the mouth." The message implored the Oklahomans to refrain from throwing "pitchforks or big heavy ears of corn" on the field during the band's halftime performance.

Oklahoma responded to the band's insults by beating the hell out of Stanford 19–7.

DALLAS COWBOY FANS

Sept. 24, 1960

The King of the Cowboys rode into town as the guest of the Dallas Cowboys, but the reception he got looked like a Redskins ambush.

Roy Rogers and his wife, Dale Evans, were the stars of a halftime extravaganza to celebrate the Cowboys' very first NFL game. But what began as the perfect promotion backfired when Roy and Dale were trashed by young Dallas fans as the western stars made their spotlighted entrance into the Cotton Bowl.

"It seemed like a great idea at the time," recalled Jim Skinner, the team's first entertainment director. "The King of the Cowboys would help kick off the first Cowboys game."

The team also invited the Hardin-Simmons University Cowboy Band from Abilene, Texas, to add to the western flair and arranged for the game to be played on Saturday night so it would attract even more attention.

That night, as the first half ended, the stadium lights were dimmed. Roy and Dale's singing group, the Sons of the Pioneers, took their places at midfield and began to croon the cowboy couple's theme song, "Happy Trails to You." Spotlights shone on the 30,000 spectators and then beamed toward one end of the Cotton Bowl where Roy and Dale, decked out in their full rhinestone regalia, appeared perched on the back seat of a white Cadillac convertible.

The pair waved and smiled to the crowd as the convertible slowly circled the field.

"Right away, we started seeing stuff flying out of the stands as the car went by," Skinner recalled. "People were throwing ice, cups, all sorts of stuff at them.

"As the car made the turn and came down the main stretch in front of the press box, Roy was beating on the driver's shoulders and screaming, 'Get us out of here!'"

The driver, Tom Hughes, stepped on the gas and the car lurched forward, with Roy and Dale grabbing for handholds while they frantically ducked the ice barrage.

When the driver reached the 50-yard line, he stopped and opened the car door. But Roy refused to leave the car.

"Finally, Tom had to literally drag him out," Skinner said. "Roy went to the microphone at the center of the field and proceeded to really berate the crowd. It got quiet as a church while Roy blasted away about how he didn't appreciate the way they were treating him and his wife."

Pointing to the end zone seats where rambunctious young fans were sitting, he said, "I want you to know I'm mad at some of those kids down there." Taking their cue from the singing cowboy, a posse of Dallas cops swarmed into the stands and hauled 43 little buckaroos off to the hoosegow for throwing cups and ice. They were all later released to their parents.

Following Roy's tirade, the now subdued show went on.

"Roy said he'd never come back to Dallas again," Skinner said. "Nobody was singing 'Happy Trails' after that. We thought he would be among friends, but it looked like the King of the Cowboys had ridden into the middle of a Washington Redskins huddle."

COLUMBIA MARCHING BAND

1965–Present

No band has gone more out of its way to get booed than the Columbia Marching Band. To the outrage of many, the zany collection of high steppers has lampooned mom, the flag, and apple pie.

Over the years, the band has maintained a tradition of being offensive, outlandish, and off the wall. Said Lyle Zimskind, the band's 1989 drum major and scriptwriter: "We definitely make an effort to instill this tradition in freshmen. It's our responsibility to offend whomever we can get away with. Outrageousness is the only reason for existing. We'll take a dig at anything."

To prove that there are no sacred cows, the band picked the 1989 season opener at Harvard Stadium to ridicule every major issue of the day—the war on drugs, Senator Jesse Helms' opposition to pornography, and the proposed constitutional amendment prohibiting flag-burning.

Fans booed when the band formed a mock flag-burning. After simulating a flag with red and blue streamers, the band played "Light My Fire" while orange streamers "burned" the flag and members collapsed in a heap of ashes.

The skit was dedicated to the U.S. Constitution. While the mock flag went up in flames, the band announcer pronounced it as "a salute to the Bill of Rights, soon to be overturned by a legislative body near you."

That performance drew the ire of veterans' organizations and triggered "a couple of bomb threats," Zimskind shrugged. "But we're used to that. I tell critics that we're not your father's marching band."

Prominent politicians discovered that was true when the band marched (more or less) into the heart of a Democratic stronghold in 1988 and proceeded to ridicule two native sons and party stalwarts.

The scene was Harvard Stadium in Cambridge, Massachusetts. In skits poking fun at Sen. Edward Kennedy and Gov. Michael Dukakis, band members first drove an imaginary car off a bridge labeled Chappaquiddick and then formed a set of bushy eyebrows.

Zimskind shrugged off the criticism leveled at the band by those who think Columbia should fit the mold of college bands everywhere. The band is revolted by any comparisons to the precision-marching, squeaky-clean bands from such big-time schools as Michigan, Texas, or USC.

"Those kind of bands are nothing but fascists," Zimskind added.

The band's reputation for obnoxious performances was sealed on Children's Day, 1967, in New Haven, Connecticut, with a routine at halftime of the Yale-Columbia game that graphically depicted various birth control methods.

Columbia's marchers later updated that sex-show theme during the computer virus scare in 1988. The virus originated with a Cornell University graduate student, so the band devised a routine for the Cornell game combining computer technology with the Surgeon General's safe sex warning.

"We did a show about avoiding the virus," Zimskind said. "We demonstrated how to use a surge protector whether you have a 3½-inch hard drive or a 5½-inch floppy, and announced that you should always use a modem on your Wang.

"We formed a surge protector that some people thought was not unlike a phallic symbol. We had people wearing white run up the length of it, which could suggest anything. When they got to the top they were repelled by the protection at the tip."

Sometimes, the band gets a little too clever for its own good. One year, at Holy Cross, the band performed a routine in which Christians were thrown to the lions. When they left the field and the game resumed, the Holy Cross Crusaders mauled the Columbia Lions 77–28.

POOP TALKS

Pep talks are designed by coaches to inspire their teams and to infuse their players with the desire to go beyond their limits. Too often, however, the coaches are the ones who go beyond the limits—of taste, propriety, and zeal. There should be a penalty for illegal use of the tongue. For "The Zaniest Pep Talks Ever Given," The Football Hall of SHAME inducts the following:

O. J. SIMPSON

Running Back ■ Buffalo Bills ■ Nov. 17, 1974

In a rousing halftime pep talk, O. J. Simpson tried to fire up his Buffalo Bills teammates by urging them to kick some butt. But the only butt that was kicked in the second half was the Juice's.

Most of the time, Simpson was best known for his quiet leadership in the locker room. But sometimes, when things were going against Buffalo, he took over the halftime oratory and produced some stirring speeches that would have made even Knute Rockne sit up and take notice.

But when he tried to incite the Bills to knock the Dolphins out of commission during a critical game in Miami, the pep talk backfired right in his face.

Late in the 1974 season, the Bills were tied with the Dolphins for first place in the AFC Eastern Division with identical 7–2 records. When the two teams clashed in the Orange Bowl, Miami ran all over Buffalo in the first half and was on its way to taking over first place in the division.

AP / WIDE WORLD PHOTOS

During halftime, O. J. stood up in front of his discouraged team-mates. "Hey, even if we lose," said Simpson, "we can go out and beat these guys up physically. Then maybe they'll lose some later games and we can catch up to them. Let's go out and really hit!"

Coach Lou Saban recalled that one of O. J.'s special targets was Dolphins linebacker Nick Buoniconti.

"Nick was always giving O. J. fits," Saban said. "He was one of the few guys in the league whom Juice really had trouble running against. So when we went back out after halftime, everybody was looking to put some hurts on Buoniconti.

"We got the ball at the start of the half and on the second play I heard O. J. yelling: 'Oh, Nicky! Where are you? Here I come! Ooooooooeeee!'

"And the next thing I heard was Buoniconti going: 'Here I am, Joooooce! Come and get me!'

"We ran the play right at Nick. There was a big collision and the guy down at the bottom of the pile didn't get up for a minute or two.

When he did, I saw that it was O. J. He came limping off the field and wasn't worth a damn the rest of the game. But Nick was still out there tearing us up."

Guard Reggie McKenzie anchored the offensive line in front of O. J. and usually cleared a path for the Juice to flow.

"We played hard every game," recalled Reggie, "but after O. J.'s talk we went out for that second half with a little extra snap. When I saw O. J. limping off the field, I thought, 'Oh, no! That's not the way we diagramed that play.' Then I looked around and there stood Buoniconti, healthy as a horse and grinning like the cat who ate the canary."

Simpson's pep talk not only flopped, but it also failed to help the Bills' title hopes. They lost to the Dolphins 35–28. And Buffalo, with a strained Juice, never did regain first place. The Bills split their next four games while Miami went 3–1 and won the division.

AMBUSH OF THE PALEFACES

When Pop Warner coached the Carlisle Indians—a team of Native Americans—he'd try anything to motivate his players.

Minutes before a 1917 game against Army at West Point, Warner gave one of his shortest and cleverest pep talks ever. He simply told his players, "Just remember. These are the boys who took your land."

Carlisle slaughtered Army 28–0.

LEN CASANOVA

Coach ■ Oregon Ducks ■ Nov. 14, 1964

Oregon coach Len Casanova ranted and raved at his team for so long during one halftime tirade that no one had a chance to go to the bathroom before the start of the second half.

That was no big deal for most of the players with strong bladders. But it was hell for kicker Dave Tobey. He had to pee so badly that twice on kickoffs he dribbled the ball only 15 yards.

Although Tobey was nearly incapacitated by Casanova's long-winded diatribe, it all turned out for the best thanks to a lucky bounce of the football.

During halftime of a 1964 game against Indiana, Tobey was squirming in agony. He was trying to hold his bladder while Casanova went on a verbal rampage that seemed to go on forever—especially for the Oregon Ducks' placekicker.

"Cas was such a gentleman, he rarely raised his voice," recalled Tobey. "But when we came in at halftime behind 21–7, he was really irate. Cas went into a tirade and I didn't think he was ever going to stop. I had to go to the bathroom, so I got up to go to the can."

Casanova yelled at Tobey to sit down. Cas had a lot more to say and the tongue lashing continued. Tobey bit his lip and struggled manfully to hold his water. By the time Cas was finished, an official was ordering the Ducks back onto the field, so Tobey didn't get to relieve himself.

He also had to kick off to start the second half. Due to his waterlogged condition, Tobey approached the ball with a stiff-legged gait and, predictably, squibbed the kick. The ball traveled 15 yards and bounced out of bounds.

"We drew a penalty and had to kick again," said Tobey. "On the second try, I was really going to boom it out of there. I had visions of the ball sailing out of sight. But I was shaking so badly from trying to hold it in and not wet my pants in front of 20,000 people that I shanked the ball again.

"Only this time it bounced off an Indiana lineman. One of our guys recovered it for an onside kick that surprised us as much as it did them."

While Tobey dashed to the locker room to finally relieve himself, the Ducks quickly drove for a score. Oregon's surprise kickoff recovery and touchdown turned the game around as the Ducks racked up 22 unanswered points in the second half to beat the Hoosiers 29–21.

"You know the old saying: 'For lack of a horse, a kingdom was lost,'" said Tobey. "Well, this one is: 'For lack of a pee, a game was won.' It sounds totally bizarre, but if I had been allowed to go to the bathroom at halftime, we probably wouldn't have beaten Indiana."

Afterward, Casanova was credited with brilliant coaching for ordering an onside kick. Perhaps it had something to do with a sideline conversation Tobey had with Casanova upon returning from the bathroom. "Ah, coach," whispered Tobey. "If anyone asks, can you say we planned that onside kick?"

Cas grinned and replied: "I don't think we have any choice. Who's going to believe the truth?"

PAT O'BRIEN

Actor ■ Hollywood ■ 1939

During the filming of a big scene, actor Pat O'Brien's re-creation of Knute Rockne's famous "Let's-win-one-for-the-Gipper" pep talk was a bit too stirring.

The actors who portrayed the Notre Dame football team were so moved by O'Brien's speech that they totally lost their heads. They charged out of the movie-set locker room in a frenzy—and knocked down the walls!

"I bet Rockne himself didn't have the effect Pat O'Brien had on us," recalled Nick Pappas, one of the extras on the set of the movie *Knute Rockne: All-American*. "We went roaring out of there ready to whip everything in sight. We forgot it was just a movie and not the real thing."

Pappas, a former tailback at the University of Southern California, was one of the players who acted in the football scenes in the movie that starred Ronald Reagan as George Gipp.

The halftime scene following the death of Gipp took place on a Hollywood sound stage. The actors portraying Gipp's Notre Dame

teammates were gathered in the movie-set locker room when O'Brien, as an ailing Rockne, entered in a wheelchair.

"They had him made up to look just like Rockne and he had the voice down pat," Pappas said. "He gave this tremendous pep talk to a bunch of players who had been through a lot of such talks.

"O'Brien sounded so convincing that he got me and the other actors all fired up like it was a real game. When Pat O'Brien got to that part about winning one for the Gipper, I had tears in my eyes. I jumped up and screamed, 'Let's go!'

"The other guys charged with me and we knocked down all the fake scenery as we got out of there. Then we remembered where we were. It took a couple of hours to put the set back together so we could reshoot the scene. We really believed we were going out to win one for the Gipper."

Bill Radovich, a USC guard who also played in the NFL, was one of the other extras. After the excitement died down, the tough veteran whispered to Pappas that he knew it was a fake all along and that O'Brien's fiery speech hadn't affected him.

"He just didn't want to admit it, but Rad was the first guy through the wall," Pappas said.

ROBERT ZUPPKE

Coach ■ Illinois Fighting Illini ■ Nov. 17, 1934

Before one particular big game, Illinois head coach Robert Zuppke figured the best way to loosen up his team was to kiss off his usual pep talk. But it proved to be the costliest pregame psych job of his illustrious career.

Zuppke, who in 29 years of coaching Illinois compiled a remarkable record of 131–81–13, was trying to figure out a way to pump up his undefeated but weary team for its 1934 game against Wisconsin. The Illini had won all six of its previous games and were gunning for the Big Ten conference championship with a win against the underdog Badgers.

When the Illini arrived in Wisconsin, they were mentally and physically exhausted because the starters had played both offense and defense with few substitutions throughout the entire season.

The night before the game, Zuppke came into the room of quarterback Jack Beynon and said, "We're really beat up physically, and I don't know whether I can get the boys up for the game tomorrow."

Beynon nodded in agreement.

"Well, I'm going to have to think of something to get all of you mentally prepared," sighed Zuppke. "But for the life of me I don't know what I'm going to say."

The day of the game, Zuppke decided to take a gamble. After the Illinois players put on their uniforms, they noticed, to their consternation, that they hadn't seen the coach in the locker room. Everyone's knuckles began turning white. Game time was fast approaching and the coach was nowhere in sight. Who was going to talk to them? Who was going to fire them up? Who was going to give them last-minute instructions?

Just moments before the team was slated to run out onto the field, somebody threw open the locker room door. There was Zuppke standing outside laughing and joking with some friends. He stopped in the middle of a sentence, stuck his head into the locker room, and said to his boys, "Well, if you guys can't beat this team, there's nothing I can say to help you." Then he turned around and continued his lighthearted conversation with his friends.

The players sat stunned at first. Then they broke out in laughter. "I'd never seen Zup more relaxed," recalled Beynon. "Unfortunately, that's the way we played. We were too relaxed and we really didn't get going until too late in the game."

Wisconsin whipped Illinois 7–3 on a second-quarter interception that was returned for the lone touchdown. It was the Illini's only loss of the year and prevented them from winning the conference championship. From then on, Zuppke always gave an impassioned, fiery pregame pep talk.

HE GOT THE CHAIR

In a pregame pep talk in 1963, East Mississippi Junior College coach Bob Sullivan was his usual animated self.

For added emphasis, he flung a chair toward the door. Unfortunately, an assistant coach picked that precise moment to open the door and declare, "They're ready for us."

The assistant wasn't ready for the chair, though. It hit him square in the jaw and knocked him out cold.

DAN DEVINE

Coach ■ Notre Dame Fighting Irish ■ Sept. 15, 1975

Before his first game as Notre Dame head coach, Dan Devine was so nervous in the pregame pep talk that he diagramed plays of a former team—and the Fighting Irish didn't have the foggiest notion what he was talking about.

"Now I know why they were confused," said Devine. "I was giving them plays I'd used with the Green Bay Packers. The poor kids just sat there scratching their heads."

Devine had followed a successful 13-year coaching career at the University of Missouri with a not-so-successful stint as head coach of the Packers. After he left Green Bay, Devine went where few coaches have gone before—to fill some big shoes at Notre Dame.

When he moved to South Bend, Devine decided to learn the numbering system of the Notre Dame plays rather than introduce a whole new set of plays.

"It was a tough adjustment for me," recalled Devine. "But I decided those kids had enough to do getting used to a new coach. I thought it would be easier if I learned their numbering system. That was my mistake."

The two systems were opposites. If one number designated a right sweep in college, it meant go left in the pros. Devine was still trying to sort out the two different systems when Notre Dame went east to play Boston College in the season opener.

"Everybody had the pregame jitters," said Devine. "I think I was more nervous than anyone, but I tried not to show it. I talked to the kids about how the game was important because it was the first of the season, it was my first as head coach at Notre Dame, and we were in Boston playing Boston College for the first time."

Without being too theatrical, Devine also spoke briefly of how it was now their turn to carry on Notre Dame's winning tradition. Then he turned to the chalkboard and began outlining offensive plays and game strategy.

But the plays Devine was describing might as well have been written in Sanskrit. Nobody—except Devine—had ever seen them before. The puzzlement mounted until an assistant coach discreetly corrected Devine. "Uh, Coach," he said, "don't you mean 37 instead of 67?"

Devine looked at the board and suddenly realized that while he'd been talking to the Notre Dame players, he had been using the old Green Bay plays. He quickly switched gears. Suddenly everything made sense to the Irish, who then went out and beat Boston College 17–3.

"The kids were too polite to say anything while I rambled on," said Devine. "I pretended like nothing had happened. But it was probably my most embarrassing moment."

ED McKEEVER
Coach ■ Notre Dame Fighting Irish ■ Nov. 11, 1944

With his team trailing 33–0 at halftime, Notre Dame coach Ed McKeever asked himself what the legendary Knute Rockne would have told his players in this same bleak situation.

Then it dawned on McKeever. He'd follow the same course of action as Rockne—he'd lie through his teeth.

During the one year he spent at the Irish helm, McKeever was dazzled by the legends of Notre Dame coaches Rockne and Frank Leahy. He swore that when his time came, he'd join their ranks with his own stirring pep talk.

He had his chance against Army in 1944. The Cadets were No. 1 in the country, and although the Irish were ranked in the top 10, they were hopelessly outmanned and the Irish were getting clobbered when they trudged into the locker room at halftime. But McKeever mounted his soapbox and whipped out his crying towel. Grandma McKeever, the coach said, choking back a sob, had been stricken the night before and wasn't long for this world.

With crocodile tears streaming down his face, McKeever mournfully told the squad how much Notre Dame football meant to the poor old thing. And now that Ed, her favorite grandson, was the head coach of her beloved Irish, she could pass on happily just knowing that his team had beaten Army.

But at this late stage, he added, even a couple of touchdowns might be enough of a psychological boost to pull her through. Grandma's fate rested on their shoulders, McKeever told the team.

But Notre Dame players had been weaned on stories of similar scams perpetrated by former Irish coaches. The most famous of the lot was when Knute Rockne read a bogus telegram supposedly from his critically ill son, Billy, pleading for "Daddy's" team to beat Georgia Tech. The Irish did. When Notre Dame returned to South Bend, the first to greet the team was none other than Billy himself—in picture-perfect health.

Now the Irish were listening patiently to another made-up sob story, this time from McKeever. Unfortunately, his theatrics failed to work.

"McKeever picked the wrong bunch to pull it on," recalled George Ratterman, sophomore backup quarterback on the 1944 team. "We'd all grown up on those Notre Dame stories and it just went in one ear and out the other."

Late in the game, with the score 59–0, Irish quarterback Boley Dancewicz—despairing that his team couldn't even make a first down, much less a touchdown—stumbled into the huddle and wondered aloud what play to run next.

A battered teammate shrugged. "It doesn't make any difference," he told Dancewicz. "The old bat must be dead by now."

She was.

"We found out later McKeever's grandmother had been buried eight years earlier," said Ratterman.

WILD CARDS

Every team has at least one—an eccentric who's like a loose ball that no one can handle. In the gridiron of life, he was born on the 51-yard line. He's a card, a flake, an off-the-wall kook who defies convention and sometimes his coach. And the card is always a king—of comedy. For "The Daffiest Characters of the Game," The Football Hall of SHAME inducts the following:

TIM ROSSOVICH

Defensive End–Linebacker ■ Southern California Trojans–Philadelphia Eagles–San Diego Chargers ■ 1965–73

To straitlaced coaches, Tim Rossovich was a threat to the republic. To everyone else, he was an impetuous flake, a zany madcap in helmet and shoulder pads.

Teammates were wary of Tim. He wore a giant hedgerow hairdo and a Dracula cape. He ate lighted cigarettes and chewed glass beer mugs. He occasionally set himself aflame as a joke and once ran into the streets with nothing on but shaving cream.

Rosso or Timbo, as he was nicknamed, probably would have been run out of football had he not been a hard-hitting 6-foot, 4-inch, 240-pound All-Pro defensive end and linebacker.

When Rossovich arrived at the University of Southern California, the coaches knew he was no ordinary freshman. He put dents in all the lockers by ramming them with his head. His campus capers were so wild and frequent that he spent as much time in the dean's office as in the locker room.

School officials took a dim view of Tim's indiscretions, which to him were nothing more than innocent life experiences. Once, Rosso

stripped naked and lathered himself with shaving cream from head to toe. Then he ran outside and waved at passing motorists.

Another time, after taking a shower, Tim walked out onto an eight-inch ledge of an upper-floor window at the dormitory and stood there nude in broad daylight. When the dean demanded an explanation, Rossovich replied, "It was a windy day. It seemed like a good way to dry off."

Tim got into further trouble when he and his wackier pals bought old cars for $25, parked them in the middle of Los Angeles intersections, and then destroyed them by using sledgehammers or by setting them on fire.

Rosso's fraternity, Sigma Chi, was eventually put on social probation due in part to his antics. "We used to throw bottles at each other in the halls," he recalled. "There always seemed to be about six inches of broken glass on the floor and two guys at the health center getting stitched up."

But the prank that really raised the hackles of the dean occurred when Tim and his fraternity brothers filled the hotel elevator with water. When the door opened, the water went *swoosh* into the lobby.

The Philadelphia Eagles were willing to overlook all of Rossovich's shenanigans to make him their No. 1 draft pick in 1968. Perhaps it had something to do with the fact that Tim was co-captain of USC when it won the national championship in 1967 or that he was an All-America defensive end.

Tim quickly made a name for himself in his rookie year. He and Eagles teammate Mike Ditka (who later became coach of the Chicago Bears) engaged in a bottle-opening contest—using only their teeth. It was no match. Rosso opened 100 bottles to Ditka's three. To celebrate, Tim quaffed some beer—and polished it off by eating the beer mug.

Rosso graduated from chewing glass to consuming lighted cigarettes and live spiders. Then he did his postgraduate work in incendiary acts that would rival those of any self-respecting arsonist. Tim would set himself on fire!

His zaniest blaze happened when he made a flaming entrance at a party hosted by Steve Sabol, who now heads NFL Films. Rossovich doused himself with lighter fluid, lit a match, and then knocked on the door. When the door was opened, there stood Tim in flames. "Oh, God! He's on fire!" screamed the guests. "Somebody do something!"

On fire from head to toe, Tim walked into the room, where two guests saved him from being too well done by knocking him to the floor and smothering the flames with blankets. Once the fire was extinguished, Rossovich got to his feet and looked casually around the room. Then he announced, "Sorry, I must have the wrong apartment," and walked out.

"He had it all figured out," said Sabol. "He could burn up to 40 seconds without injuring himself. The thing at the party was a put-on. Two of his pals waited 30 seconds before extinguishing the flames. He'll do anything for a laugh."

To liven up a birthday party for a teammate, Tim went into the bathroom, took off his clothes, and, with a mighty croak, came leaping out and into the living room like a huge frog. Then he did a back flip and landed bare assed in the birthday cake.

The Eagles front office frowned on Rosso's antics. The conservative bigwigs and coaches believed Tim wasn't a proper role model because he looked and acted like an antiestablishment weirdo. In fact, they ordered him to cut off most of his long bushy hair and to cool it on the capers. He grudgingly had his hair clipped, but he refused to stop goofing off. If anything, he acted even zanier.

He loved to go into the training room and make death-defying leaps into the team's whirlpool tank, which was only the size of a washing machine. All his teammates laughed, except the poor guy who was already in the tank when Tim made his dive.

One time, during an important team meeting, Rosso stood up to address his fellow Eagles. Stretching his arms wide to make a point, he opened his mouth, and out flew a baby sparrow. Another time, the players were getting dressed for a game when an Eagle shouted, "Hey, look at Timbo!" Everyone turned around. There was Rossovich with his head tilted back with something white and furry squirming in his mouth. It took a few seconds before the players realized that Tim had stuffed his mouth with the head of Mouser, the albino clubhouse kitten.

Rossovich often arrived for games dressed in clothes right out of central casting. If he was in a western mood, he wore buckskin; if in a cosmic mood, he donned psychedelic shirts and overalls that said "Unidentified Flying Object." Sometimes he came draped in a Dracula cape or walked around in a wizard's outfit and wore Aladdin shoes that curled up at the ends and had bells on them.

On road trips, Rosso carried a compass because he always slept with his head pointed north. "That way," he explained, "magnetic waves can flow through my body and revitalize me." Tim was known to sleep only four hours a night—on the floor, face down. This sometimes caused anxious moments for hotel maids who would walk

HARD-HEADED

Hall of Famer Bronko Nagurski earned his reputation as "Hard Rock" when he played fullback for the Chicago Bears from 1930 to 1937.

Once in a game at Wrigley Field, the Green Bay Packers stopped the Bronk three times inside the 5-yard line. Infuriated, he set himself for one all-out plunge for the touchdown. He crashed through the line, bounced off two defenders, and, with his head still down, smashed into the goalpost and caromed into a brick wall behind the end zone.

Accepting the congratulations of his teammates, Bronko said, "I took some good shots, but nothing compared to that last guy. That's the hardest hit I've ever had."

in and find a naked man lying face down on the floor. They'd think he was dead.

They already knew he was zany. More than once they saw Rosso suddenly carry out a strange urge to stand on his head in the lobby—sometimes with his head in a bucket of water.

Tim loved to put people on. One day at Rittenhouse Square in Philadelphia, Rosso found a big box. He dragged it out into the middle of Walnut Street, crawled inside, and curled up. When people stopped and asked what he was doing in there, Tim replied, "We had a tough practice today and I'm relaxing."

Then there was the time Timbo walked into a Philadelphia bar with a cast on his arm and told the patrons that he had broken it during practice earlier in the day. About a half hour later, he got into an argument and began pounding the bar with the arm on which he wore the cast. He worked himself into such a frenzy that he smashed a chair with his arm and pieces of plaster from the cast flew in all directions. The stunned patrons stared at Rossovich, knowing there was no way a man with a broken arm could destroy a chair like that. Timbo looked shocked, too. Suddenly, he held up his arm, and in mock rapture shouted, "My God, I'm cured!"

RON McLEAN

Defensive Tackle ■ Cal State–Fullerton Titans ■ 1983–86

Ron McLean loved his football gear so much he slept with it!

At night, he tenderly laid his equipment out on the bed beside him so it could get a good night's sleep before a game.

"I always pretended my gear was alive and it was playing the game with me," said the 6-foot, 4-inch, 260-pound tackle. "Guys would ask me what my equipment was doing on the bed and I'd tell them it was resting up for the big game."

Throughout his playing career at Cal State–Fullerton, McLean went through a ritual of laying out his gear, starting with the helmet and going all the way down to the cleats.

The helmet went on the pillow. Next came the shoulder pads clad in the game jersey with the gloves in the end of the sleeves, followed by the hip pads, thigh pads, knee brace, pants, ankle wraps, socks, and finally the shoes at the foot of the bed.

"When I was done, it looked like a real person," said McLean. "When my gear was all ready for bed, I laid down beside it and went to sleep.

"People kidded me about sleeping with my equipment, but I didn't sleep with it on. I slept beside it. When we woke up in the morning, we were both rested and ready to go out and play. It was a closeness I felt with my gear. We understood each other."

But McLean's love affair with his equipment didn't end there. On weekends and in the off-season, he spirited it out of the locker room and took it home so it wouldn't be lonely.

During the summer, McLean often donned his gear and went to a nearby park to block and tackle the trees.

"Since there weren't any blocking dummies nearby, I practiced on the trees," recalled McLean. "Most of them were stripped of bark by the time I got done. I'd give out a bloodcurdling scream and slam into some poor tree until the ground shook. It scared the hell out of all the little kids and old people who hung out in the park."

Since the Cal State–Fullerton campus was just down the road from Disneyland in Anaheim, opponents discovered they could drive McLean to his wacky extremes by deriding him about playing for "Cal State–Disneyland."

"It made me crazy when people teased me about playing on a Mickey Mouse team," McLean said. "At Colorado State, some joker hung a Mickey Mouse doll in effigy from our goalpost. I went into a frenzy and ripped it to pieces.

"Another time at Fresno State, a reporter wearing a set of Mickey Mouse ears came into the locker room. He started making cracks about us being a bunch of goofy characters from Disneyland. I screamed, 'I'll show you goofy!' and grabbed the ears, threw them on the floor, and jumped up and down on them until I squashed them.

"Somebody got it on tape and I ended up being the star on television that night. But it was on the news. Not *The Mickey Mouse Club*."

JOHN McNALLY
(AKA JOHNNY BLOOD)

Halfback ■ Milwaukee Badgers–Duluth Eskimos–Pottsville Maroons– Green Bay Packers–Pittsburgh Pirates ■ 1925–38

Johnny Blood was the NFL's original swashbuckler.

He was so cocky that he often dropped easy passes on purpose and then caught the impossible ones. When running with a clear field ahead, he'd deliberately slow down until pursuers could catch up to him—and then he'd break away.

Off the field, Blood was as unpredictable as a tornado—and just as wild. He lived as if there were no tomorrow. In fact, he'd risk his life to pull a prank or prove a point. An All-Pro hell-raiser, Johnny broke training rules and curfew with the same reckless abandon that he displayed breaking tackles and records.

And to further set himself apart from any other pro who ever donned a helmet, Johnny had a penchant for signing his autographs in blood—his own!

UPI / BETTMANN NEWSPHOTOS

Despite all his capers and clowning, Blood helped lead the Green Bay Packers to four NFL championships. He was such a dynamic runner and pass catcher that he was elected a charter member of the Pro Football Hall of Fame.

On and off the field, Johnny did what he wanted, when he wanted—including changing his name. Born John McNally, the gifted athlete, scholar, and poet was playing football for St. John's University in Minnesota when he decided to also join a local pro team. But to keep his college eligibility, he needed an alias. He and a teammate, who also was looking for a second name, were walking in downtown Minneapolis when Johnny spotted a movie marquee that read "*Blood and Sand*, starring Rudolph Valentino."

"That's it!" said Johnny, pounding his friend on the back. "We've got our names. I'll be Blood and you'll be Sand." While Sand drifted into oblivion, Blood became one of the NFL's zaniest and best players in the 1920s and '30s.

Big leads bored him so much that he deliberately turned easy plays into hard ones. "Johnny always made the difficult play for you," said teammate Ernie Nevers, captain of the Duluth Eskimos. "It was what he did with the easy play that disturbed us. If we were ahead, he'd sometimes drop passes thrown right to him. Or else, if he was loose on a touchdown run, he'd slow down and lateral to a less swift teammate."

During one Eskimos game against the Chicago Cardinals, Blood broke away on an 80-yard run with no one in front of him. But that wasn't any fun. So he wanted to lateral to a teammate. But when the Cardinals reached Johnny first, he started zigzagging, waiting to lateral. He edged closer to the goal line as the Cardinals pursued him until, to his disgust, Johnny had to score the touchdown himself.

Another time against the Buffalo Rangers, Blood ran 60 yards en route to a touchdown. But since this presented no challenge for him, he waited at the 5-yard line for three pursuers to catch up with him. Then he dragged all three over the goal line.

Playing for the Packers in a game against the New York Giants, Blood took a lateral from quarterback Red Dunn and scampered 45 yards for a touchdown. The next time they ran the same play, Blood had an open field ahead of him. But he playfully threw the ball back to the surprised Dunn, who was then smothered for a five-yard loss.

Johnny's antics were just as audacious off the field.

During the Packers' train ride home after clinching the 1930 title,

Blood laughingly threw wet towels at his teammates. He nailed end Lavie Dilweg in the back of the neck. With a roar, Dilweg chased Blood through the entire length of the train. When Johnny reached the last car, Dilweg shouted, "Now I've got you cornered!"

But Blood coolly opened the door, stepped onto the rear platform, and climbed on top of the moving train, where he ran along the roof, leaping from car to car until he reached the engine. There he joined the startled engineer and fireman and rode with them to the next stop.

Johnny would go to any length to prove a point. Once, he and Eskimos teammate Joe Rooney got into a deep discussion over who was tougher. So they agreed to go out into the alley and duke it out. "They weren't sore at each other," explained Nevers. "No, they were just curious. And we couldn't stop them. They fixed the door so nobody could come outside to stop the fight. Only the winner was to return."

About 15 minutes later, Blood and Rooney returned arm in arm with their bruised faces and tattered clothes splattered with blood. "It was a tie," declared Johnny. But he had broken several bones in his right hand. Nevertheless, he played the next day.

Risking life and limb meant nothing to Blood. Once in the lobby of the Packers hotel, he asked coach Curly Lambeau for a small loan. Lambeau, knowing that money burned a hole in Johnny's pocket, refused. "I won't even advance you ten cents," said the coach. "Now I'm going to my room and lock myself in for the night. So don't bother coming to my door because I won't let you in."

But Blood was not to be deterred. He went to the eighth floor and stepped outside into a driving rainstorm and onto the fire escape. Then he hopped onto the ledge. However, Lambeau's room was across an eight-foot-wide courtyard. So Johnny simply leaped across the chasm onto the ledge outside the coach's room, lifted the window, and stepped inside as a stunned Lambeau clutched his heart.

"I thought that perhaps I didn't make myself clear, Coach," the dripping-wet Blood said matter-of-factly. "About that advance I asked for . . ."

Lambeau pulled out a wad of bills and stammered, "Take it! Take it and go! And don't ever do that again!"

"Thank you, Coach," Johnny said politely. "I knew we'd come to an understanding once we talked things over."

Lambeau did everything he could do to control Blood except put him in a straitjacket. Because Johnny loved wine, women, and song as much as football, he had no use for curfews and training rules. As a result, Lambeau fined him so often that Blood usually owed the team money.

"Johnny was the most fined man in pro football," Lambeau said. "But he never complained, whether it was for $25 or $200. He'd just say, 'I had it coming, Curly,' and pay."

During contract negotiations in 1929, Lambeau offered Blood $100 a game, providing he would initial a clause in the contract forbidding any drinking from Tuesday until after the game on Sunday of each week. Johnny accepted the $100 a game, but only if he could drink after the Sunday game through Wednesday. Curly agreed.

Although the agreement curbed Johnny's imbibing, he couldn't quench his thirst for women—especially those who always seemed to get him in trouble.

One beautiful young Chicago woman was so smitten with Blood that she followed him to San Francisco. Johnny felt he should do something special for her. So, when she asked for his autograph, he cut his forearm with a razor blade, dipped a pen in his blood and signed his name. But Johnny had cut himself too deeply. Blood squirted everywhere and he was rushed to the hospital where a dozen stitches were needed to close the gash. Nevertheless, he played the next day.

A few years later, Johnny risked his life and the possible derailment of the Packers' train for a woman with whom he had spent the night. "It was simply an obligation I had to a young woman," he told the

YOU GET WHAT YOU PAY FOR

During practice the week before the New York Giants played the Los Angeles Rams in 1953, New York coach Steve Owen drilled defensive back Emlen "The Gremlin" Tunnell on how to stop future Hall of Fame receiver Crazy Legs Hirsch.

"Above all, don't let him get by you," Owen pleaded.

With the Rams leading 14–7 late in the fourth period, Hirsch put a nifty move on Tunnell, caught a pass from Norm Van Brocklin, and raced into the end zone for the clinching touchdown.

When Tunnell returned to the bench, Owen stormed, "Why, why, why did you let Hirsch get past you?"

Tunnell replied, "Coach, he gets $18,000 a year. I get $8,000. He's supposed to get past me."

press. "She was a late riser, which put great demands on chivalry. Anyhow, the Packers train was leaving at 10 A.M. and I got a late start for the depot and discovered the train had left without me. There was really no choice. Either I stopped the train, which was then just pulling out of the yard, or I'd get fined for missing it."

Blood zoomed ahead for three blocks and then swung his car across the tracks a couple of hundred feet in front of the train. Said Johnny, "I couldn't imagine that the engineer was a callous man and would run the engine through the car—especially since the lady and I were still in it." The train screeched to a halt only a few yards from the car. Blood then gallantly turned the wheel over to the young woman, kissed her goodbye, and boarded the train.

His teammates weren't surprised. After all, he was Johnny Blood.

JACK "HACKSAW" REYNOLDS

Linebacker ■ Los Angeles Rams–San Francisco 49ers ■ 1970–84

According to football legend, Hacksaw Reynolds acquired his nickname because he got mad once and went out to the parking lot and sawed his Jeep in half.

"That's not true," said the 6-foot, 1-inch, 230-pound linebacker. "I never sawed a Jeep in half. I love Jeeps. I owned six of them one time.

"It was a '53 Chevy that I sawed in half."

One might think that Reynolds came by the nickname for the way he cut down opposing runners during his 14 years as a middle linebacker with the Rams and the 49ers. But he picked up the moniker during his senior year at the University of Tennessee when he came, he sawed, and he conquered.

The story about the Jeep was mistold so often that Reynolds finally had hundreds of flyers printed up entitled "The Hacksaw Story" and passed them out to set the record straight.

In 1969, the Volunteers had only to get by Mississippi to wrap up the Southeastern Conference title and an invitation to the Sugar Bowl. But Ole Miss totally embarrassed the Vols with a 38–0 shutout.

"I was so frustrated over the licking we took that I just had to do something," recalled Reynolds. "After the game, I went up on a big bluff overlooking the river. There was an old car up there, a 1953 Chevrolet, with no motor."

For reasons he can't explain, all of Reynolds's anger and disappointment over losing the big game focused on that piece of junk. He went to the nearest K-Mart store, loaded up on a supply of hacksaw blades, and set to work rearranging the Chevy's design.

"I sawed it behind the door jamb between the front and back seat, right on down through the drive shaft," said Reynolds. "I started it Sunday afternoon, but I had to go back Monday morning to finish it. The metal would bind on the blade and that made it hard to saw. It took me eight hours in all, and I used up 14 hacksaw blades doing it."

Tuesday morning, Reynolds returned with some of his teammates to recover the back half of the Chevy and use it to make a trailer for his Jeep. But both halves had already disappeared. "To this day, I don't know what happened to them," said Reynolds. What did happen that day was that Hacksaw had a new nickname that stuck with him throughout his football career.

"That was one of the crazier things I've done," Reynolds admitted. "I was just so frustrated over losing that I had to do something. I guess I'm just an eccentric."

GET ME TO THE CHURCH ON TIME

During the 1925 season, Chicago Bears end Duke Hanny asked Coach George Halas for permission to skip an upcoming game so he could get married.

Halas understood the priorities in life—football came first. The coach refused the request and demanded that Hanny suit up for the game. Duke knew if he played, he couldn't possibly make it to the church on time because it was in Rockford, Illinois, a three-hour drive from Chicago. But if he didn't play, he could be blackballed. So Hanny arrived for the game—and unveiled a crafty plan.

On the opening kickoff, Duke ran up to the nearest defender and cold-cocked him. The referee immediately threw Hanny out of the game. Happily, Duke raced off the field, got dressed in his finest duds, and sped off to Rockford to get hitched.

LARRY "THE WILD MAN" EISENHAUER

Defensive End ■ Boston Patriots ■ 1961–69

Larry Eisenhauer was nicknamed The Wild Man for good reason—
because he was.

Before games, Larry punched holes in locker room walls with his
head, flattened teammates on the sidelines to psych himself up, and
once even charged out of the locker room wearing nothing but his
helmet.

"I was known as the class clown," said Eisenhauer, "but everything I did was controlled insanity to keep everybody hanging loose. I was a very emotional player and did a lot of stuff to psych myself up for the game."

Most of the things he did were at the expense of the equipment or his teammates' health. Before a game, Eisenhauer routinely demolished the locker room. He slammed lockers until the metal doors bent on their hinges and he kicked benches and baskets across the room.

His favorite tactic was to picture the face of the opposing quarterback on the locker room wall. After concentrating on the image for a few minutes, Larry would let out a bellow and attack the wall like he was sacking the quarterback.

The Wild Man became so crazed imagining the face of Buffalo Bills quarterback Jack Kemp that he smashed open a hole in the locker room wall when he charged into it head-on.

"I really couldn't do as much damage as I intended because the room was too small to get up a good head of steam," recalled Larry. "The hole was only as big as my helmet."

If he couldn't find a convenient wall to bash, Larry settled for one of his own teammates. Pacing the sidelines during one game, Eisenhauer became so emotional that he whacked Ron Hall on the shoulder hard enough to put the defensive back out of commission.

"Another thing I liked to do was run off the field right after the pregame introductions and blast one of our guys as hard as I could," Eisenhauer said. "It got so that everybody was running and ducking as soon as I was introduced because they didn't want to get hurt.

"Finally, they assigned one guy for me to hit—Lenny St. Jean, an offensive guard who was built like the Incredible Hulk.

"He loved getting hit. The other guys set him up to take my shots so they wouldn't have to. It got to be a ritual. I'd run off the field after being introduced, look for Lenny, and give him a hard shot. After about five years, he finally wore me down. He was such a solid guy I couldn't budge him."

Larry was always on the lookout for ways to fire up the other Patriots while he was psyching himself up. During a game against the Chiefs in 1966, The Wild Man pulled one of his most outrageous stunts.

The Pats needed to win all their remaining games just to stay in contention with Buffalo for the Eastern Division lead in the old AFL. Boston arrived in Kansas City right on the heels of a blizzard.

"I wanted to do something to really inspire our guys," said Eisenhauer. "So while we were starting to suit up, I just grabbed my helmet, yelled, 'Let's go, gang!' and ran out the door with nothing else on. I meant to go all the way out, but the wind was really blowing and everything was like ice.

"I got as far as the top of the steps leading to the field and that was enough for me. When I hit that cold air I came back down real fast! I may have been crazy, but not stupid. But it did loosen everybody up and we tied the Chiefs 27–27, which was almost as good as beating them that year."

Larry's actions spoke as loudly as his words. Once during a road game in 1965, he walked up to teammate Jim Colclough, a 185-pound wide receiver, and thundered, "Jimmy, that's the ugliest sports coat I have ever seen!" With that said, Eisenhauer ripped the colorful jacket clean up the back. By the time Colclough recovered from the shock, Larry had handed him $100 to buy a new coat.

Another time, the team had a couple of hours to kill in a motel before their bus took them to the airport. The rooms had already been cleaned, but the manager told the players they could use some of the rooms to watch television if they kept the rooms neat. "For God's sake," implored the manager, "don't mess up the beds."

That's all Eisenhauer had to hear. Like an avenging angel, he ran from one room to another, stripping every bed. The team was fined for each room he messed up.

Larry sealed his reputation as a wild and crazy guy when he conned his dad into skinny-dipping in a motel swimming pool during a road trip to San Diego.

ONE-EYED JOKER

Kansas City Chiefs All-Pro end Fred Arbanas was once hit so hard in a 1965 game that his glass eye popped out.

Referee Tommy Bell picked up the fallen eye, handed it back to Arbanas, and said, "Fred, you've got a lot of guts. What would you do if your other eye was injured?"

Arbanas didn't even crack a smile as he replied, "Mr. Bell, I'd become a referee just like you."

"My dad's nickname was Big Dutch," Larry said. "He stood 6 feet, 5 inches tall and weighed 300 pounds. He came along on that trip and wanted to go swimming at the motel. I told him the outside pool was a little too cold, but there was this one inside that was heated and would be just the thing for him. I conned him into believing that since it was a private pool he could go skinny-dipping."

One wall of the pool was actually a huge window behind the Mermaid Bar, the motel's cocktail lounge, where the patrons were waiting for an underwater ballet performance by scantily clad water nymphs.

Eisenhauer then went around alerting the Patriots that a special show in the Mermaid Bar was about to begin.

"The place was packed," recalled Eisenhauer. "But instead of a dainty little ballet with girls in bikinis, they got Big Dutch who looked like some great white whale flopping around in the water. He belly-flopped into the pool, scratched his balls, and swam over to the glass and tried to look out. It was like a one-way mirror. He couldn't see anything, but we could see him and everyone in the place was cracking up."

Everyone, that is, except the motel manager, who called the cops when he discovered the naked sea monster in his pool.

"We talked them out of charging Dad with indecent exposure, but it was pretty embarrassing," said Eisenhauer. "Dutch laughed when he found out I'd conned him. But I don't think he ever went swimming again."

ART DONOVAN

Defensive Tackle ■ Baltimore Colts ■ 1953–61

Art Donovan was named to the Football Hall of Fame for his great defensive skills. But they were nothing compared to his Football Hall of SHAME achievements—like gobbling 25 hot dogs at a time, doing a striptease at weigh-ins, and scolding opposing quarterbacks in their own huddle.

The 6-foot, 3-inch, 270-pound defensive tackle loved two things in life—football and food, especially hot dogs.

"I could go down to Coney Island any day and stand there and eat 25 hot dogs," recalled Donovan. "If I was pressed, I could eat 50. Maybe only 35 kosher-style."

Usually, it was an even dozen. The only discomfort Art experienced afterward was his embarrassment over going back and ordering a dozen more to eat. But he solved that dilemma by calling over a teammate and saying, "Here's the money. I'll wait right here and you go buy them for me."

Donovan ate a very simple diet—cheeseburgers, Spam, pizza, and, of course, hot dogs. "I'm a light eater," he once said. "I never start eating until it gets light."

Throughout his career, Art seemed to gain weight just by looking at food. So the front office put a clause in his contract stipulating that he had to weigh in every Friday morning at no more than 270 pounds or face a $1,000 fine.

Said Donovan, "I'd have dinner on Monday, and then I wouldn't eat until Friday after weigh-in." But then he would pig out. "By Saturday I'd weigh 280."

Art turned his weigh-ins into a performance worthy of stripper Blaze Starr. Recalled teammate Dick Szymanski, "Arthur knew how we all enjoyed watching him make weight. He'd make a real show out of it. He'd get on the scale wearing his socks, shorts, and undershirt and then jump off before we could see what the scale said. He'd take off his socks and get back on. He'd jump off again and remove his shirt. Then off would come his shorts and finally his false teeth and he'd be right at 270 where the club wanted him."

One time the striptease didn't work. Two days before a big game against the Rams in Los Angeles in 1959, Donovan tipped the scales at 272 pounds.

"Coach [Weeb Ewbank] said that if I had a good day, he'd think about lifting the fine," recalled Art. "In the second half, we busted the game open. But it was 105 degrees and I was dying. With a couple of minutes to go, the Rams sent in a rookie quarterback, some kid I never heard of. He was running all over the field. I was chasing him and screaming at him, and calling him all sorts of names. I finally had to do something about it.

"I marched right over to the Rams' huddle and told the kid quarterback, 'Just settle down and run out the clock or I'll kill you.' He must have known I couldn't catch him on a motorcycle because he looked up and said, 'I hope you drop dead, Fatso.' " (The young quarterback was Frank Ryan, who five years later led the Cleveland Browns to an NFL championship.) Because the Colts won big that day, Donovan wasn't fined.

To Art, practice and fitness were a joke. "I did 13 pushups in 13 years," he said. "I once told Weeb, 'Do you want a gymnast or do you want a football player?' The only weight I ever lifted during my career was a beer can."

As a runner, Donovan was so slow the Colts used him as a measuring device to cut rookie linemen. During the rookies' first day in training camp, Coach Ewbank put them in a foot race against Donovan. "If they couldn't beat me, they were on the next train out of camp," said Art. "One day I beat two of them. We never saw either again."

One of Donovan's more memorable Hall of SHAME moments came during a 1955 game against the Rams. Los Angeles quarterback Norm Van Brocklin had just called an audible, causing a shift in the Baltimore defense. Colts middle linebacker Dick Szymanski quickly ordered Art, "Hey, move over, Fatso. You're in the wrong position." So Donovan moved. But seconds later, after thinking that Szymanski was mistaken, Art shouted back, "Syzzie, you sonofabitch, you're wrong. You move." So Szymanski took up a new spot and Donovan went back to his original position. But then Szymanski had second thoughts and told Donovan, "You fat idiot, no. You're wrong. You move back."

Meanwhile, on the other side of the line of scrimmage, an incredulous Van Brocklin halted his count as he watched the two buffoons shout back and forth. Finally, the Ram yelled at them, "I can't believe this. When you two idiots get straightened out, I'll start playing." Then, to everyone's surprise, Van Brocklin called time out and stalked off the field.

Donovan secured his niche in the Hall of SHAME early in his career when the Colts were staying at the Beverly Wilshire Hotel in Beverly Hills. Art had never seen stall doors on a combination tub and shower. So he got this great idea. He hopped in the tub, closed the doors, turned on the bath water, and let it rise almost to the top of the doors. Then he swam around—until the stall doors burst open. A river of bath water cascaded into the bathroom and flooded the room below, damaging the carpeting and furnishings.

Donovan never tried swimming in a hotel tub again.

ALEX KARRAS

Defensive Tackle ■ Detroit Lions ■ Dec. 16, 1962

Life in the trenches for Alex Karras was nothing but one big blur. His eyesight was so bad he used to claim, "I play football by Braille."

Karras wasn't that blind. But his batlike vision led to one of his most embarrassing moments ever on the gridiron.

The "Myopic Monster" refused to wear glasses or contact lenses when he played because, he said, he was a better lineman when he had to play blind.

No one wanted to get in the way of a 6-foot, 2-inch, 250-pound, ferocious, charging lineman—especially one who had trouble telling the difference between a teammate and an opponent. Or between his own brother and another player.

During a 1962 game against the Chicago Bears, Karras didn't need glasses to see that it was a bitterly cold day and a boring game. "We were doing what we always did when we were losing and it felt like it was 40 below zero," Karras recalled. "We were trying to find some way to get out of there and get warm."

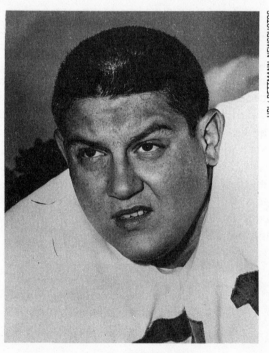

Bears offensive guard Stan Jones, who was lined up across from Karras, provided Alex with an opportunity. "Stan was terrible about holding," said Karras. "In this game, what he was doing to me was so obvious and illegal that I really got angry. I decided that the next time it happened, I was going to punch him. Not just to get even, but in hopes the ref would see me and throw me out of the game so I could end all the misery."

On the next play, Alex leaped on the blurry form across the line, unleashed a couple of hard punches and, for good measure, delivered a swift kick to the foe's head.

"Alex! Alex!" cried the downed player in the Bears uniform. "What the hell are you doing to me?" Karras detected a familiar ring in the voice. Then the roughed-up player shouted, "I'm your brother!"

Karras got down on his knees, peered closely at the prostrate figure, and discovered he had been beating up his older brother, Ted Karras!

Ted normally played left offensive guard and since Alex usually played left defensive tackle, the brothers rarely faced each other across the line. But on this particular play, Chicago coach George Halas had moved Ted to Stan Jones' spot.

"Of course, Alex, with his poor eyesight, couldn't tell who I was," recalled Ted. "And I didn't know he was laying for Stan. So after I nailed Alex with a good solid block, he started pounding me. Then he gave me a kick to the head.

"I was yelling at him, 'For God's sake, Alex! I'm your brother! You shouldn't do that to me.' But he just stared at me and then walked away."

A few days later, when the Bears were reviewing film of the game, the play in which Alex mugged Ted appeared. Halas took great delight in running the scene over and over for the amusement of the Chicago players.

"Take a look at this," said Halas, pointing to the movie screen. "This is what you call brotherly love? He kicks his own brother's teeth out."

Alex didn't go that far, but he did leave a lasting impression on Ted—a black and blue one.

Despite the embarrassment of unwittingly beating up his own brother, Karras still refused to wear glasses or contacts on the field. "[Detroit Lions] Coach George Wilson made me wear contacts once," said Alex. "It scared me to death when I saw all those big fellows running at me. I put the lenses away after two games. I could play better when I didn't know what I was up against."

THE FUMBLE FOLLIES

You can tell who they are by looking at their fingers—they're all thumbs. These players are the maladroit bumblers who carry the ball as if they are allergic to pigskin. Their muffs often trigger a rash of boos and jeers that stay with them longer than the ball. For "The Most Embarrassing Fumbles Ever," The Football Hall of SHAME inducts the following:

JOHNNY LATTNER

Halfback ■ Notre Dame Fighting Irish ■ Oct. 18, 1952

Notre Dame star Johnny Lattner fumbled the ball so many times during one big game that his coach made him do public penance the following week—Lattner had to walk around campus toting a football with a handle on it!

Coach Frank Leahy came up with the offbeat punishment after Lattner fumbled five times in a 1952 game against previously unbeaten Purdue. As a reminder to hold on to the pigskin, the coach gave Lattner the special handled football and ordered him to "go to the chapel and repent for those five mortal sins you committed on Saturday."

"He meant it," said Lattner, the Heisman Trophy winner in 1953. "To Coach Leahy, any mistake you made on the football field was a sin against Notre Dame. And during that Purdue game, I made a bunch of them. He made me carry the ball around all week so the Notre Dame students would see it and shame me into not fumbling again."

But Lattner wasn't the only one who couldn't hang on to the ball that day. His five fumbles were among 21 in the game as an epidemic

of butterfingeritis swept through the Purdue and Notre Dame squads.

"We were just getting used to the split-T formation, so our timing on the handoffs was out of whack," recalled Lattner. "That was our excuse. I don't know what Purdue's was, but I do know I'll never forget Leahy's reaction."

Even though Notre Dame won 26–14, the Irish coach was stunned by all the fumbles and could barely speak following the game. But by the time the squad had gathered for a team meeting on Monday morning, Leahy had regained his voice.

"Leahy didn't say anything to me directly," Lattner said. "But during the team meeting he started telling a story about a young player who had disgraced himself by fumbling five times.

"He went on to describe how this nameless player had also disgraced his teammates, his coach, and his school. He had disgraced his friends and his family. He had disgraced the Blessed Mother. He had disgraced his own father. Even though my dad was dead, Leahy managed to work that in somehow."

After the lecture, the rest of the team was given the day off. But not Lattner. Leahy sent the chastised star out to the field with an assistant coach.

A rope was strung horizontally between the goalposts at waist level and Lattner spent hours taking handoffs from the coach and ducking under the rope.

"I was the only player out there," Lattner recalled. "I must have ducked under that rope 1,000 times or more. Finally, I was so worn out, I just ran into the rope face first and broke the rope."

But Leahy had more punishment in mind. He gave Lattner a special football attached to a handle taken from an old valise. The coach told Johnny to carry the ball with him everywhere he went for the next week.

"I carried that ball to chapel, to meals, to practice, and to class," said Lattner. "I was afraid not to. Leahy may have been joking, but I wasn't taking any chances. Other than some finger-pointing and smiles, no one said anything to me. If I hadn't done what Leahy told me, the punishment would have been even worse.

"But it didn't do much good. The next week against Michigan I fumbled three times!"

CHARLIE DALE

Announcer ■ Harvard Stadium ■ Oct. 4, 1975

Charlie Dale holds a shameful distinction as the only stadium announcer ever to cause a fumble.

Dale's boo-boo that led to the bobble came during Harvard's 13–9 loss to rival Boston University.

Across town, at Fenway Park, Boston's beloved Red Sox were locked in a critical American League playoff game with the Oakland Athletics. As the football and baseball games progressed, Dale kept the faithful at Harvard Stadium posted on developments at Fenway with periodic updates on the score.

Meanwhile, the Harvard Crimson struggled against the underdog BU Terriers. Harvard backs fumbled eight times during the game and lost the ball on four of those occasions, so they didn't need Dale adding to their woes. He did anyway—unwittingly.

Late in the game, Harvard was faced with a third down and seven at the BU 33-yard line. Crimson quarterback Jim Kubacki hoped to catch the Terriers off balance with a play that called for center Carl Culig to snap the ball on the first sound he heard following the quarterback's "Set!" command.

Kubacki got under center and called "Set," but then spotted something in the BU defense he didn't like. He stepped back and started to raise his hands to signal time out.

Up in the booth, Charlie Dale picked that very instant to announce to the waiting crowd, "Red Sox 7, Oakland 1!"

Culig, being the good center that he was, snapped the ball on the first sound he heard. Unfortunately, Kubacki had already moved from his position.

"I was pulling out when Carl snapped the ball," recalled Kubacki. "It hit my leg and popped about eight feet straight up in the air.

"We had been having problems holding on to the ball all day. Everybody was on edge and Carl was sort of the nervous type anyway, so we sure didn't need that outside interference."

Kubacki fell on the ball, but lost a critical down. The Crimson failed to gain a first down and the ball went over to BU, which held on for a 13–9 upset victory.

"After the game, the coach told us to tear that play out of our playbooks," recalled Kubacki.

GREEN BAY PACKERS

Oct. 15, 1984

The Packers suffered one of the quickest and most embarrassing series of fumbles ever when they coughed up the ball on their first two plays from scrimmage and spotted Denver two easy touchdowns.

It took only 37 seconds for the Broncos to rack up the Pack in a 1984 Monday-night game that started with a blizzard of Packer miscues and a Rocky Mountain snowstorm that nearly obliterated the field. More than two inches of snow covered the ground and it was still coming down at game time.

The Broncos won the opening coin toss. But with the tricky winds and snow swirling through Mile High Stadium, Denver coach Dan Reeves decided to kick off first and unleash his defensive unit on the Packers.

Reeves guessed right. On the first play of the game, Green Bay halfback Gerry Ellis took a handoff and plunged into the right side of the line. The ball squirted away like an icy snowball. Bronco safety Steve Foley scooped up the ball at the 22-yard line and went slipping and sliding into the end zone for the touchdown.

After the extra point, the Broncos kicked off again. On the first play of their second possession, the Pack came back with an instant replay for the TV fans who tuned in late and missed the first fumble. This time it was fullback Jessie Clark who couldn't find the handle on the ball.

Just as Clark hit the right side of the line, most of the Broncos plowed into him. The ball popped out in front of cornerback Louis Wright, who gladly gathered in the ball and rambled 27 yards for the second score in less than a minute of play.

Former Green Bay great Forrest Gregg was in his first season as Packer head coach. "Naturally, it had to happen during a Monday-night game when the whole world and all my old teammates were watching," Gregg moaned. "At first, I tried to blame it on the weather. The truth is that it was just an old-fashioned case of the butter-fingers."

"I've never seen anything like that before," Foley said. "I went out there on the third series ready to get another one."

He didn't get the chance. Green Bay runners managed to hang on to the ball during their third possession. After 5½ minutes of playing time had elapsed, the Bronco offense finally got a chance to play. They should have stayed on the bench. John Elway and company scored only three more points the rest of the game, but still managed to hang on for a slippery 17–14 win.

KOSHER FOOTBALL

Syracuse running back Dick Fishel gave 110 percent but also gave his coach, Vic Hanson, heart failure by carrying the football like a loaf of bread.

Playing against Colgate in 1935, Fishel dove over the goal line for an apparent touchdown, but he fumbled the ball and Syracuse lost possession and eventually the game.

Later in the locker room, Hanson read Fishel the riot act. "For God's sakes, all year long we've stressed that you're supposed to hold on to the ball with two hands. How in the hell did you ever drop that ball in the end zone?"

Fishel stared back at Hanson and said, "Didn't you figure it out, Coach? The football is made of pigskin. I'm Jewish. I had to drop it."

GRANT FEASEL

Center ■ Seattle Seahawks ■ Oct. 22, 1989

In one of the wackiest fumbles of the 1989 season, center Grant Feasel snapped the ball during a field goal attempt—and bopped the holder on the side of his head.

The botched attempt cost Seattle a chance to tie the Denver Broncos, who eventually won by a three-point margin. The Broncos finally won by a three-point margin, 24–21.

"That was kind of typical of our 7–9 season," said an embarrassed Feasel. "It was just a mental lapse that cost us a shot at tying the game and maybe winning it later."

In the second quarter on fourth down at the Denver 18-yard line, Seahawks kicker Norm Johnson came on to try the field goal. Reserve quarterback Jeff Kemp was the holder.

As Seattle lined up, Kemp looked over the Denver defense and spotted what looked like a blitz formation. He cupped his hands and yelled to the Seahawk linemen, "Watch it, left!"

"Jeff was just doing his job," recalled Feasel. "But I wasn't doing mine. I thought he said, 'Red set,' which is the signal to snap the ball quick so I let it go."

Unfortunately, Kemp had turned his head back to Johnson to repeat the blitz warning to him when Feasel snapped the ball. It smacked Kemp on the side of his helmet and bounced straight up. Kemp fell on the ball, but since it had been fourth down, Denver took over possession.

"When I went home after the season, that play was the only thing my friends wanted to talk about," lamented Feasel. "They thought it was hilarious, but it wasn't funny to me.

"But we've corrected the problem. I won't be snapping the ball into Kemp's earhole again without making damn sure that's where it's supposed to go."

LEN DAWSON

Quarterback ■ Kansas City Chiefs ■ Nov. 15, 1964

No player suffered a more severe case of fumblitis than Len Dawson.

The Kansas City Chiefs' Hall of Fame quarterback played as if the affliction were terminal—he set an ignominious NFL record by fumbling an incredible *seven* times in one game.

Two of his bobbles halted scoring drives. Even worse, two more of his fumbles led directly to touchdowns for the San Diego Chargers in a span of just 56 seconds. And those scores proved to be the difference in a 28–14 Chiefs loss.

Dawson contracted fumblitis from a torrential downpour that turned the field in Kansas City into a quagmire. His symptoms were obvious to everyone—he couldn't hold on to the snaps from center.

"I never really had hold of the ball on any one of the fumbles," recalled Dawson. "I was diving for the ball the whole first half. It was raining so hard the water was going up my nose. One time, I almost drowned when I got hit and they buried my face in a puddle of water."

Dawson's worst moments with the dropsies came in the second quarter. With his team trailing 14–0, Dawson fumbled the snap on the Kansas City 47-yard line. San Diego recovered and on the next play, Chargers quarterback John Hadl hit wide receiver Lance Alworth for a 47-yard touchdown pass.

On the first play after the kickoff, the ball squirted out of Dawson's hands again on the snap and was recovered by San Diego, this time on the Chiefs' 19-yard line. Before Dawson had time to lament the muff, Alworth scored his second touchdown within less than a minute, giving the Chargers an insurmountable 28–0 lead.

"I couldn't control the ball on the snap from center and I couldn't figure out why," said Dawson. Hadl wasn't having a problem with the exchange. Then Dawson noticed that the San Diego center was gently handing the ball to Hadl. So Dawson asked his center, Jon Gilliam, to snap the ball softly.

"I only dropped a couple more balls after that," said Dawson. "But I still got tagged for those seven fumbles and a place in the record book—which somebody reminds me of every year."

During practice a few days later, Kansas City coach Hank Stram decided Dawson needed to practice in the mud. He ordered the groundskeeper to make a huge mud puddle in a corner of the practice field. "Coach Stram had our equipment manager tape thumbtacks on my fingers and then clip the points down as close as possible," said Dawson. "Then he made me and Gilliam go out in the mud puddle and practice snaps all day. I was able to grip the ball pretty good, but those tacks sure tore it up.

"We never used the thumbtacks in a game because it never rained like that again. They were illegal anyway—but that wouldn't have made any difference to Stram."

HITTING THE OPEN MAN

George Ratterman, Notre Dame's backup quarterback on the 1946 championship team, tossed only one interception that year. It happened during a game against Southern Cal.

Trying to widen a 26–0 lead, Ratterman heaved the ball far downfield where a USC defender leaped high in the air, intercepted the pass, and returned it 15 yards.

When Ratterman reached the sidelines, Notre Dame's interim coach, Moose Krause, demanded, "Why in heaven's name did you throw the ball to that Southern Cal back?"

Ratterman's reply was frank and to the point: "Shucks, Coach, he was the only man open."

The media has done a remarkable job covering football from every angle possible. However, sometimes the best stories focus not on the players but on the members of the press. Sportscasters, reporters, and photographers have done some pretty silly things while covering football games. For "The Most Outrageous Press Coverage of Games," The Football Hall of SHAME inducts the following:

KEITH JACKSON

Sportscaster ■ ABC-TV ■ Nov. 16, 1970

The *Monday Night Football* action on the field was hot, but it was even hotter in the broadcast booth. Play-by-play man Keith Jackson was burning up the airwaves while a small fire was burning up his pants.

"I've had some pretty uncomfortable times in the booth," Jackson recalled. "But that really had me sweating—in more ways than one!"

Monday Night Football was in its first season. Millions tuned in to the weeknight telecasts of NFL games to hear Jackson, along with Howard Cosell providing the pomposity and former Dallas Cowboy Dandy Don Meredith delivering the one-liners.

What those millions didn't see or hear on this Monday night from the Cotton Bowl were Jackson's frantic efforts to douse a blaze that had set his pants on fire—while he was describing the action on the field.

"We were really under a magnifying glass for that game," Jackson recalled. "First, there was all the attention on *Monday Night Football* in its first season. Second, there was a big deal made about it being Meredith's first time back to Dallas as a broadcaster.

"In those days, everybody smoked. I smoked. Don even smoked a little. And, of course, Howard smoked like a chimney all the time. In a game like that, with a lot to keep track of, you keep throwing notes and things away and by the third quarter there are a lot of papers and debris piling up under your feet.

"Somehow a cigarette fell on the floor and apparently smoldered there for a while unnoticed."

About the same time, a brouhaha erupted on the field. St. Louis Cardinals quarterback Jim Hart, scrambling for a first down, took a late hit out of bounds. Cardinals piled on Cowboys, fans in the stands were on their feet yelling, and Hart was rolling around on the ground in agony.

Meanwhile, up in the booth, "Howard was pontificating and Meredith was waving his arms and shouting," said Jackson. "I suddenly felt something hot and looked down to discover my pants were on fire.

"The cuff had caught fire and it was spreading fast. I grabbed everybody's Cokes, water, or whatever else they were drinking and poured it all over my britches trying to get the fire out and still describe the action down on the field.

"I probably sounded like a damn fool and I imagine all those people watching must have wondered what in the hell was going on. After about a minute I managed to douse the fire without it burning me, but I sure ruined a good pair of pants.

"One of the things I remember most about it now is that I sure didn't get any help from my partners. Don was cracking up and rolling around on the floor. Howard was jumping up and down and screaming for someone to call the fire department. I had to put out the fire all by myself."

JOE COLOGNORI

Photographer ■ *Richmond Times–Dispatch* ■ Sept. 27, 1947

Joe Colognori was awarded a football letter when he snapped a picture that helped win a game. But it was an honor he could have done without.

The letter was bestowed on him by archrival Washington & Lee University after one of Joe's flashbulbs blinded the defenders on his hometown team, the University of Richmond, and paved the way for a Washington & Lee victory.

As he did for all the Richmond Spiders games, Colognori was prowling the sidelines during a Saturday-night clash between his favorite team and the Generals. He was armed with a flash camera to get the best possible action photos for his newspaper, the *Richmond Times-Dispatch*.

Late in the second quarter, Richmond took a 3–0 lead with a field goal. On the kickoff, Washington & Lee running back Brian Bell caught the ball on his own 15-yard line, cut to his right, and picked up his blockers.

"When I got to midfield, Mike Boyda was running interference for me right down the sideline," Bell recalled. "There were only two defenders left between me and a touchdown.

"They had the angle on me and were moving in to cut me off. The photographer was standing alongside the bench and shot off a flash just as I ran past him. It went off right in the eyes of the two Richmond players just as they were bearing down on me."

A split second before attempting their tackles, both defensive backs were blinded by the sudden flash. Unable to see, they mistook Boyda the blocker for Bell the ball carrier.

While Boyda was buried by some textbook gang tackling, Bell deftly sidestepped the confusion and raced untouched for the go-ahead touchdown. Washington & Lee eventually won the game, 16–3.

Later that year, the Washington & Lee athletic council awarded the cherished W&L monogram to Joe Colognori for helping the Generals win the game.

A PREGNANT PAUSE FOR THOUGHT

Sportscaster Curt Gowdy made a classic blooper during the telecast of the AFL All-Star Game. Noting that a downpour had formed a small lagoon on the playing field, he told viewers, "If there's a pileup out there, they'll have to give some of the players artificial insemination."

FRED "CUBBY O'SWEITZER" DRYER

Defensive End

LANCE "SCOOP MULLIGAN" RENTZEL

Wide Receiver
Los Angeles Rams ■ Jan. 6–12, 1975

Los Angeles Rams Fred Dryer and Lance Rentzel bamboozled the Super Bowl IX teams and the press by posing as a pair of daffy reporters.

Team members quickly caught on to the put-on and had a good laugh, but NFL officials weren't amused.

Even though the Los Angeles Rams lost the 1974 NFC Championship game to the Minnesota Vikings, Dryer and Rentzel went to the Super Bowl anyway. They donned some 1920s duds straight out of the movie *The Front Page* and arrived in New Orleans as credentialed reporters.

UPI / BETTMANN NEWSPHOTOS

"We're here to spread as much hearsay and innuendo as we can," announced Rentzel, clad in a pinstripe suit, a bow tie, black-and-white brogans, and a wide-brimmed floppy hat bearing a red "press" card. "Covering the Super Bowl is a great thrill. Can we be bought by either team? Yes!"

Presenting a card that said, "Scoop Mulligan, Reporter," Rentzel introduced Dryer around as "Cubby O'Sweitzer." Dryer, who carried a camera that had seen better days, was attired in a gangster suit with a vest, a green Andy Capp hat, and a tie wide enough to use for surfing.

The two first showed up at the Pittsburgh Steelers' hotel where they interviewed running back Franco Harris (see photo). Then they attended the team press conference where coach Chuck Noll was answering questions. Midway in the session, Rentzel asked Noll, "Do you think the zone defense is here to stay and if not, where'd it go?"

Noll, by now used to stupid questions from the press, didn't realize the query was a put-on nor did he recognize Rentzel. So the coach proceeded to give a detailed explanation of the merits of the zone defense.

Rentzel and Dryer asked a few more inane questions before a league official scolded them for turning the press conference into a sham. The fourth estate's dynamic duo then headed over to the Vikings' press conference.

There, they started in on Vikings defensive end Jim Marshall. "Does skull size indicate IQ, and if so, why?" Dryer asked him.

"Oh, man, this is too much," replied Marshall.

Rentzel then butted in and told Dryer, "Rewrite that, Cubby. It's not good enough."

Then Dryer asked Marshall, "Do you prefer grass . . ."

"Man, you shouldn't be talking like that!"

". . . or do you prefer Astro-Turf?"

Another league official broke up the interview to admonish the pair in front of the other reporters. When the room fell silent, Rentzel said, "The press is depressed."

But not for long. The two headed to a far corner of the room where they ganged up on quarterback Fran Tarkenton, who became a willing victim. The dialogue went like this:

DRYER: "Strictly off the record, Fran, is the Super Bowl just another game?"

TARKENTON: "I'm just happy that we're going to have a chance to play in it. I'm just so happy that I'm going to kick [Steelers defensive lineman] Joe Greene's butt."

RENTZEL: "Mark that down, Cubby. Tarkenton threatens Greene's life. Now, Fran, have you ever jumped offside?"

TARKENTON: "Only when I gave Fred [Dryer] the fake move in the game last week."

DRYER: "Is it true, Fran, that you're unable to win the big one?"

TARKENTON: "That's a true statement. I don't have the dedication to come up with the big play in the big game."

RENTZEL: "Rewrite that, Cubby, and punch it up. Now Fran, can you still throw with your sore arm?"

TARKENTON: "Absolutely! In practice yesterday, I was able to throw the ball 15 yards. I believe that was the longest pass of my life."

RENTZEL: "After the Vikings win the Super Bowl, what are your plans?"

TARKENTON: "To meet the winner of the Punt, Pass, and Kick Contest."

Later, Rentzel was asked about Dryer's journalistic ability. "I think he's going to be a great reporter. For one thing, he won't pay for anything. He needs coaching on how to pad his expense account. But I think he can be bought, so there's talent there. If he doesn't like the answers he gets, he'll rewrite them or make up new ones. He's good at starting rumors."

Dryer patted Rentzel on the back and said, "I'm very grateful. I've learned so much from Lance."

NBC'S TELECAST OF THE POINSETTIA BOWL

Dec. 20, 1952

For a game in which hardly any fans had shown up, NBC Sports enlisted the Navy's Shore Patrol to rustle up enough warm bodies to provide a decent crowd shot.

In 1952, NBC Sports was faced with a major public relations crisis. A crew that included play-by-play announcers Tom Harmon and Lindsey Nelson was set to telecast the first annual Poinsettia Bowl nationwide. It was a major sports event in those early days of television and one that was eagerly awaited by millions of football fans across the country.

But an unexpected deluge threatened to wash the site of the game—San Diego's Balboa Stadium—out to sea. Six hours of steady downpour had flooded the streets and forced cancellation of the city's Poinsettia Parade and the pregame festivities.

The game, for the so-called national service championship, pitted Bolling Air Force Base against the "hometown" San Diego Naval Training Center. Even for a game as meaningless as this, several thousand tickets had been sold.

But when the rains came, the fans didn't. They stayed home by the thousands, opting instead for the rare opportunity to see a game televised from their own city.

As they looked around the drenched and nearly empty stadium, the NBC honchos and Poinsettia Bowl boosters panicked. They suddenly realized they were about to go on the air coast to coast—and the only thing millions of viewers would see would be row upon row of deserted seats.

The bigwigs at NBC Sports and the bowl officials sent out a frantic call to the Navy brass to do something. The network cameras absolutely must have a crowd to show the country, or else the San Diego image—and the Navy's—would sink like a scuttled scow.

The Shore Patrol was issued orders and swung into action along San Diego's rainswept streets, shanghaiing sailors wherever they could find them. The Patrol raided bars, cafés, movie theaters—and those other places gobs on shore leave were apt to hang out.

Several hundred reluctant Navy and Marine recruits were gathered up, bused to the stadium, and ordered to sit together in one section in the torrential rainstorm. Throughout the game, whenever the directors needed a crowd reaction shot, the television camera focused on

UNFIT FOR A KING

Larry King, popular radio and TV personality, used to do the color on football telecasts.

Once during halftime of the Miami Dolphins–Baltimore Colts game, King announced, "Now coming onto the field to entertain the fans is the Air Force Academy Drug and Bugle Corps."

that one bunch of soaked and sullen sailors and ignored the thousands of empty seats.

One of those who was dragged from a warm, dry restaurant to be part of the contrived background was a young recruit, Hayden Fry, who went on to become coach of the Iowa Hawkeyes.

"Later, we heard we were there to play the crowd scene," recalled Fry. "But at the time, none of us knew why we were sitting there in a downpour. The Shore Patrol just picked us up, took us to the stadium, and told us to enjoy the game. Some enjoyment."

Bolling eventually won the game 35–14. But by then, not even NBC cared about the outcome and the ill-fated Poinsettia Bowl soon sank out of sight.

Training camp is a place where players are supposed to work out all the off-season kinks and fine-tune their football skills. For some teams, preseason practice makes Marine boot camp seem like a sleepaway summer camp. For other teams, getting into shape is a matter of mind over matter. Players don't mind goofing off, so it doesn't matter how silly they act. For "The Craziest Preseason Incidents," The Football Hall of SHAME inducts the following:

FRANK GIFFORD

Halfback ■ New York Giants ■ 1952

When Frank Gifford joined the New York Giants as their No. 1 draft pick, he rode in on a wave of national publicity. Story after story touted the All-America from Southern Cal as the sensational new rookie who would lead the Giants to the NFL championship.

But all those press clippings were just so much confetti to the grizzled Giants veterans. They wanted to find out for themselves just how tough Gifford was.

Frank showed them in the first intrasquad game of the 1952 training camp. The first time Giff carried the ball, he went through a big hole, cut back, took another step, and then . . . boom! . . . he was knocked out cold.

Things didn't get much better for Frank during his first week in camp. In fact, he took such a battering from the veterans that he packed his bags and headed for the door.

"The veterans were laying for Gifford just like they did with all their top picks," recalled Allie Sherman, who was an assistant coach at the time. "But Frank got it worse than most. To the old timers, he was a glamour boy. He was handsome, his wife was a beauty queen, and he was a storybook success. The veterans wanted to find out if Frank had what it took to help them win a championship, or if he was just a flash in the pan who would fold with the first hard hit."

On the first day of contact in practice, Gifford didn't leave a very good first impression with his teammates. But Giants linebacker John Cannady left a lasting impression on Frank. Cannady, all 260 angry pounds of him, had drawn the "Welcome to the NFL, Frank" assignment.

So after Gifford took his first handoff in a scrimmage, Cannady unloaded on him with a savage tackle that turned out the rookie's lights. "We wanted to see if he could take it, so I stuck him pretty good," recalled Cannady. "Frank never knew what hit him."

When Frank came to, he looked woozily up at Cannady and guard Ray Beck, who were both grinning at him. "I've never been dropped like that in my life," he moaned.

"That was just for practice," said Beck. "Wait till you get in a real game."

By the end of the week, Gifford had taken enough lumps from the Giants' welcome wagon that he could hardly walk. In fact, he was hurting so much that he was ready to chuck pro football for good.

"A couple of nights before we were to play Detroit in an exhibition game, Frank knocked on my door," recalled Sherman. "He had his bags packed and wanted to say goodbye. He said he didn't think he was doing the team any good and that the guys didn't like him very much and that he was leaving."

Sherman told Gifford that instead of feeling discouraged, he should be happy over the daily thumping he was taking from the veterans. "I told Frank that every rookie gets a rough going over and that if the older guys didn't care about him or didn't think he could take it, they wouldn't be hitting him so hard.

"I made a deal with Gifford that if he'd stay, I'd be the first to tell him if he wasn't going to make it. He agreed and then went out and played a great game against Detroit. In the locker room afterward, Frank grinned at me and said, 'I think I'll stick around a while.'"

It was a good thing he did. Gifford led the Giants to six conference titles and an NFL championship. He capped his dazzling career by being inducted into the Pro Football Hall of Fame—as well as The Football Hall of SHAME.

DOUG ATKINS

Defensive End ■ New Orleans Saints ■ 1967

Old warhorse Doug Atkins wanted a restful training camp. And to assure he got the peace and quiet he desired at night, he hauled out his trusty .38 revolver and blasted warning shots to silence those foolish enough to disturb his tranquillity.

After spending 14 years in the trenches with the Cleveland Browns and Chicago Bears, Atkins was picked by the New Orleans Saints in the 1967 expansion draft. Now in the twilight of his career, all he wanted in training camp was some quiet time after the arduous daily workouts.

The peaceful California seaside campus that the Saints chose for its first camp was just the ticket for a weary veteran of the NFL wars.

But Atkins hadn't counted on the rambunctious rookies who joined him in camp. They brought along their collection of rock music that could only be appreciated at full volume. In their dormitory rooms. Late at night.

Several times, Atkins asked them politely to turn down the music. At 6 feet, 8 inches and 270 pounds, Atkins rarely had to ask twice. But "The Big Man," as he was nicknamed, was astonished that his requests went unheeded. The young turks just blew him off with a few flippant remarks.

"I guess they thought I was just some over-the-hill old coot," he recalled.

Obviously, the rookies hadn't learned that Atkins took guff from no one—not even from the Bears' tough, no-nonsense coach, George Halas. Once during a tense game, Halas implored a bloodied and bruised Atkins, "Let's see you make a tackle!" With hands on hips, Atkins wheeled around toward the sideline and bellowed, "Damn it, Coach. If you can do any better, let's see *you* come out here and play." Halas shut up.

So Atkins wasn't about to stay silent over the noise coming from the rookies' dorm rooms on the floor above him. "I just leaned out the window with my .38 and shot a couple of rounds into the bottom of their balcony," Atkins said. "I wasn't trying to hit anybody. I just wanted to get some sleep and they were raising hell up there.

"The dormitories were sort of enclosed so the shots echoed pretty loudly. It sounded like a cannon going off and it sure got their attention. The music went off. Folks stopped talking. Even the bugs shut up.

"I had no trouble with those young boys from then on. It turned out to be a nice, restful training camp after all."

THE BLUE RIDGE RITZ

1966

The joker who named the Atlanta Falcons' first training camp the Blue Ridge Ritz was just slightly off target. The Blue Ridge Rots would have been more like it.

When the young Falcons arrived at their inaugural training site near Black Mountain, North Carolina, they were housed in a dilapidated dormitory that swayed in the breeze and threatened to collapse if anyone slammed a door. Rock-strewn fields made up the practice area. The kitchen served steaks which one rookie described as "smelling like a wet dog."

Even the Rev. Billy Graham viewed the camp as beyond hope. Graham, who lived nearby, dropped in for a visit. The famed evangelist took one look around and shook his head sadly. "I'm not sure I can help you," Graham told the players.

And the grizzled veterans, used to relieving the tedium of training camp with a few beers after practice, discovered to their dismay that they were sharing the facilities with teetotalers—a little old ladies' religious convention and an Alcoholics Anonymous retreat.

The team spent two horrendous months at the Blue Ridge Assembly facility, which was operated by the Baptist Church and was actually three camps in one. From the highway, rutted dirt trails branched off to Camp Fartherest Out on the left and Camp Last Resort on the right. The Falcons were stuck with the ramshackle camp in the middle that looked like something Dogpatch had condemned.

The paint was peeling. The creaky floors were uneven splinter factories. The windows gaped open with no protective screens to stop the daily mosquito raids. Rookie linebacker Tommy Nobis rolled over in his sleep one night and suddenly awoke to find himself hanging half in and half out of a second-floor screenless window. After that, players learned to sleep defensively.

Every morning the Falcons were rudely awakened by a rendition of "Nothing could be finer than to be in Carolina in the morning" blaring from a neighboring camp's loudspeaker. But not for long. A few days after the Falcons unpacked, the solo ended abruptly and was heard no more when a shotgun blast from the direction of the Blue Ridge Ritz shattered the Carolina morning.

When the players did stumble from their lumpy cots in the morning, they next had to face the horrors of the camp kitchen. A single mess hall ladled out the food for all three camps—except that the dietary needs of grandmas on religious retreats clashed with the ravenous appetites of 300-pound defensive linemen.

And besides being skimpy, the food was rarely edible by pro football standards. The food was so bad the players soon revolted. A spontaneous food strike began when one famished player gagged and threw his steak down. A reject-the-steak movement quickly developed as player after player followed the example until a stack of unwanted slabs of inedible beef were piled up.

An emergency meeting of the camp staff brought about some menu improvements. But mealtimes at the Blue Ridge Ritz were seldom happy times, which mystified a camp cook. "The women and alcoholics don't complain," she said.

To survive, some players and coaches had care packages of food sent from home—but at their own risk. Those who hoarded the goodies had to fend off the famished rats—both the two-legged and four-legged kinds—who came prowling at night. One time, players were jolted awake in the middle of the night by a thunderous uproar coming from Coach Norb Hecker's room. They found Hecker brandishing a broom and battling a huge rodent that was after the coach's private cache of cookies and cakes.

End Alex Hawkins was one of the 42 veterans the Falcons had taken in the expansion draft. As soon as he saw the camp, Hawkins rushed to a telephone, called Don Shula, his old boss with the Baltimore Colts, and begged to be rescued.

But for Hawkins and the other new Falcons it was too late. In an area of the country noted for its hellfire and brimstone preaching, the players faced the real thing whenever they hit the practice fields.

"I know some of the guys called the place the Blue Ridge Ritz," said Hawkins. "I called it Camp Run Amok. It was a nightmare."

Whoever laid out the site for football practice was inspired by the Marine Corps' obstacle course. It was built on two levels—an upper and a lower field. Players had to climb back and forth between fields depending on which practice drills they had to do.

"Those fields were in terrible condition," recalled Hawkins. "They came in with bulldozers, knocked down some trees, cleared a couple of patches of ground, and left us nothing but rocks to practice on. We started out with a little bit of grass, but within three weeks that was all gone.

"On top of that it rained every day for about two weeks during one period. Late in the afternoon, the sun would come out and bake the ground and us along with it."

The fields were surrounded by pine forests that cut off what light breezes there were in the humid summertime and turned the fields into open-air saunas. With the temperature and the humidity running in the high 90s, few of the 140 veterans, rookies, and free agents made it through camp without collapsing at least once.

To make matters worse, Hecker, a Vince Lombardi disciple, demanded that training sessions concentrate on conditioning. He forced players to run from one end of the field to the other in the broiling heat until they dropped like flies.

HOW I SPENT MY SUMMER VACATION

Joseph Whelan arrived from Boston College to try out as a punter for the New York Giants at their training camp in 1963. But the Giants already had All-Pro punter Don Chandler, so Whelan's chances were slim at best.

Finally, early in August, Whelan got the bad news from coach Allie Sherman. Whelan took it graciously, thanked Sherman for the chance, shook hands, and left the coach's office.

A week later, Sherman was wandering through the dorms when he discovered one light still on well past curfew. He opened the door and to his surprise saw Whelan stretched out on the bed watching TV.

"Whelan, what are you doing here?" Sherman demanded.

"Oh, hi, Coach," Whelan replied. "Listen, this is great. I didn't have anything planned for the summer. I love the food. I've made a bunch of good friends. And now I don't even have to go to practice. This is a great summer vacation."

Even Sherman had to smile. But the next day, he made sure that Whelan was gone for good.

To compound their misery, the players had to ride groaning, fume-belching buses to the practice fields a mile from camp. The road was a narrow, rocky trail. Every morning, the ancient buses bounced down the mountain with players clinging to the seats in sheer terror, since the brakes rarely worked. The drivers often stopped the buses by running into parked cars when they arrived at the practice fields.

The return trip in the afternoon was just as bad, since the buses had trouble making it up the hill under their own power. Frequently, the players were asked to get out and push—a job that was quickly delegated to the rookies.

By mid-August players who despaired of making the team were sneaking away in the middle of the night. But the Falcons insisted that the camp remain open until the regular season started in September.

On the way out of camp for the last time, Hawkins claimed, two players remained behind and set fire to the single bridge leading to the Blue Ridge Ritz. The Falcons never returned.

WAR MEMORIAL STADIUM PIGEONS
Buffalo ■ Oct. 5–7, 1965

A thousand pigeons did what rain, sleet, and snow could never do—stop a Buffalo Bills practice three days in a row. That's because smelly, messy bird droppings carpeted the field in the aftermath of a pigeon invasion.

"It stunk," recalled Coach Lou Saban. "I wanted the team to get in some extra work before an important game, but I couldn't get them to do anything except chase pigeons. None of those big, tough guys wanted to fall in that stuff."

Defensive lineman Ron McDole was one of the Bills who protested that there was nothing in his contract about practicing in bird crap. "We were going to put in some new plays," McDole recalled. "But when we hit the field for practice, there must have been a thousand pigeons grazing out there. The coach told us to get rid of them."

For 30 minutes, the Bills ran up and down the field, shouting, making noise, and waving their arms. When the players approached, the flock took off from one end of the gridiron only to settle on the other end. The Bills trudged down to the opposite end zone and resumed the chase. Meanwhile, all the excitement disturbed the birds' digestion and the field grew slicker and slimier.

Since no one was about to get down on the ground, Saban had to cancel practice. But he vowed to call up friends in high places on the Buffalo police department to remove the foul fowls.

"The next day there was a bunch of police sharpshooters picking off 1,000 pigeons one at a time while we tried to practice," McDole said. "It was nuts. Every time a cop fired his gun, some nervous lineman jumped offsides.

"Saban was pulling his hair. He couldn't get anything done and had to call off practice again."

Next, Saban sent in the health department. The experts spread poisoned seed over the field late in the afternoon. Satisfied he had the pigeon problem licked, Saban rescheduled a third workout for the following day.

"Well, when we showed up there were still about a thousand pigeons out on the field—but they were all dead!" McDole said. "In the entire time that we were supposed to be practicing the new plays, we were picking up the bodies instead. Yuck!

"Saban went ape. We never were able to get those new plays worked out."

As a result of the lost practices, the Bills weren't as prepared as they wanted to be and they lost their next game to the San Diego Chargers 34–3.

EVERY TRICK IN THE BOOK

To win at football, you need to learn the fundamentals of the game, such as hard-nosed blocking, aggressive tackling, and strong kicking. But to gain that extra edge that could make the difference between winning and losing, players need to learn the finer points—like how to make an end run around the rule book. Playing fair and square is not necessarily in their game plan. For "The Sneakiest Chicanery Ever Perpetrated by Players," The Football Hall of SHAME inducts the following:

BOB GRIESE

Quarterback ■ Miami Dolphins ■ Sept. 27, 1970

Hall of Famer Bob Griese—recognized as one of the game's brainiest quarterbacks—used his smarts to make a referee unwittingly block for him.

While eluding a sack in the end zone, the Miami Dolphins quarterback cleverly manipulated referee John McDonough into running interference for him. As a result, Griese was able to reel off a big 50-yard gainer against the Houston Oilers.

Ahead 10–3 in the third quarter of a 1970 game in the Astrodome, the Dolphins were backed up to their goal line when Griese rolled out and looked for a receiver. But everyone was covered. Meanwhile, the blocking broke down and Griese was left unprotected—except for one lone official who stood between him and the onrushing Oilers.

McDonough—better known for his whistle-blowing than for his

downfield blocking—recalled that both he and Griese were caught in the open with nowhere to hide.

"I started backpedaling as fast as I could go," said McDonough. "When I cut right, Griese cut left. Then I cut left and he cut right. On the third cut, I wiped out both guards on the Houston Oilers. I did a complete backflip and lost my hat and game card. I ended up on my knees watching Griese, who was still on his feet and running like hell down the sidelines."

Griese was finally chased out of bounds near midfield. A mortified McDonough eventually caught up with the play, but he couldn't outrun the chorus of boos from fans in the Astrodome or the angry protests from the Oilers he'd flattened.

Griese, grinning slyly over his shifty subterfuge that had kept the drive alive, then moved the Dolphins to another touchdown to seal a 20–10 victory over the Oilers.

"It's survival of the fittest out there," said Griese. "You use anybody or anything that gets between you and the enemy. I just took advantage of the situation as it developed."

At first, Griese was merely trying to avoid getting sacked for a safety. At best, he hoped to scramble for enough yardage to give his punter some breathing room. "But then along came John," said Griese. "He ran interference for me, so I sure wasn't going to tell him, 'Excuse me, sir. You're the referee. Please don't get in the way.'

"Since I didn't see any blockers wearing Dolphin uniforms, I figured that stripes were the next best thing. Fortunately for me, John threw a tremendous block or I never would have made it. The Oilers weren't happy about it, but that was their problem. Maybe it was a sneaky thing to do, but personally I was kind of proud of myself."

When the game ended, McDonough—sporting a mass of bruises as mementos of his impromptu blocking assignment—limped toward the officials' locker room where Dolphins owner Joe Robbie stopped him.

"I've been looking all over for you," Robbie told the ref. "I want to offer you a three-year, no-cut contract. We haven't had a block like that all year!"

PAUL BROWN

Coach ■ Cleveland Browns ■ Oct. 14, 1956

In a game against the New York Giants, Cleveland Browns coach Paul Brown wired his quarterback for sound so Brown could broadcast instructions to him from the bench.

But the electrifying scheme backfired—because the Giants cleverly intercepted Brown's shortwave play-calling. As a result, New York throttled Cleveland's offense and marched off with a 21–9 upset victory.

Shortly before the season started, Brown had General Electric engineer Jack Campbell develop a tiny radio receiver that could fit snugly inside a football helmet. The radio enabled Brown to stand on the sidelines with a microphone and tell his quarterback what plays to call in the huddle. It was all supposed to be hush-hush.

"We almost blew the secrecy in one of our tests," Campbell recalled. To test how far he could receive signals, Browns quarterback George Ratterman put on the helmet and walked into the woods while Campbell transmitted to him. When Ratterman failed to return, Campbell went looking for him. "George was on the road,

talking to a police officer who had picked up our signals in his squad car," said Campbell. "The officer thought he had netted some kind of nut coming out of the woods wearing a Browns football helmet."

That was the first signal that Brown's brainchild was tuned to failure.

The radio helmet was first tried in a preseason game against the Detroit Lions. Brown had even obtained a license which in effect gave him a small radio station on which he could broadcast plays to Ratterman. It didn't take the Lions long to notice Brown wasn't following his usual routine of shuttling players into the game to carry his plays to the huddle. The Lions then spotted Brown behind one of his players talking into a microphone. Next to the Cleveland bench was a transmitter and an antenna.

The Detroit players figured out his grand scheme. They also figured out the best way to deal with the situation—by bashing in Ratterman's helmet. So what if his head was still inside the helmet? The defensive line pummeled Ratterman at every opportunity, twice ripping his helmet off and pounding the inside with their fists trying to smash his receiver.

The Browns' quarterback finally exploded. He took his helmet and hurled it to the ground. "Look," he told the Lions' defenders. "You can't destroy the radio this way. It takes a lot of punishment." Obviously, they didn't get the message. They still tried to wreck his helmet—while he was still wearing it.

Besides being bruised and battered, Ratterman was also embarrassed. He looked like a fool on the field. Because he wasn't picking up Brown's signals very clearly, the quarterback had to step outside the huddle and walk in circles until he could find good reception.

The following week, during the final preseason game, Ratterman became even more frustrated. He kept receiving signals from workers who were preparing for the halftime show and communicating with their walkie-talkies. Instead of hearing Brown's play-calling, Ratterman heard, "Hey, Sam, the Navy float must go in front of the Marines and behind the Army truck."

Brown was beginning to think that maybe the radio helmet wasn't a good idea after all. He chose not to use it during the first two regular season games.

But in a home game against the underdog Giants, Brown hauled out his sideline transmitting equipment. Figuring that the Giants would try to jam his transmissions, he warned them before the game

that they faced a $10,000 fine if they loused up his signals. Because he had a licensed radio station to carry out his experiment, his sideline broadcast to his quarterback was covered by FCC rules and regulations.

The Giants had no intention of jamming his signals. They had a better game plan. They came prepared with their own console receiver, which they set up next to their bench, and tuned in to Brown's frequency.

By coincidence, the Giants had just picked up former Browns halfback Gene Filipski, who knew all of Cleveland's plays. He sat next to New York's reserve end Bob Topp, who was assigned the job of using the receiver to eavesdrop on Brown.

On Cleveland's first offensive series, Topp clearly heard Brown's instructions to Ratterman. Topp relayed the first play to Filipski, who decoded it and told Giants defensive coach Tom Landry that Ratterman was going to pitch out to the left. Landry then passed the word to his defense through sheer lung power. Sure enough, on the Browns' first play from scrimmage, Ratterman pitched out to the left—where an alerted defense was waiting. The play lost two yards.

No matter what Brown called, the Giants had the perfect defense. Finally, after three straight offensive series failed to net a first down, Brown gave up his play-calling broadcast in disgust.

Before Brown could fine-tune the radio helmet, NFL commissioner Bert Bell stepped in. He banned the use of all radio devices in football games, claiming that the only thing a quarterback should have inside his helmet is his own brains.

FLORIDA GATORS

Oct. 22, 1960

The Florida Gators took the old saying, "Finders keepers, losers weepers" to the extreme.

During a 1960 game against Louisiana State, the Gators stripped a wristband containing LSU's complete game plans from the Tigers' quarterback. Then they studied the plays and used the purloined information to storm back from a halftime deficit to win.

"It was like playing with a spy in our huddle," complained LSU coach Paul Dietzel. "The wristband showed exactly what plays we ran from each formation. With the wristband, it was simple to tell what play was coming just by looking at the formation we were in. They could narrow down the number of plays we were apt to run. And it's a whole lot easier to defense 5 plays than it is 35."

With LSU quarterback Jimmy Field calling plays written on his wristband, the Tigers effectively moved the ball throughout most of the first half. But midway in the second quarter, Field was tackled and while he was under the pileup, the Gators ripped the wristband off his arm.

"I was really upset," Field recalled. "I told the coach about it, but we didn't suspect at the time that Florida might be using it against us."

The first half ended with LSU leading 10–7. But during halftime, the Gators used the wristband to learn which plays the Tigers would run in certain situations. As a result, the LSU offense was completely stymied in the second half. Every time the Tigers ran a play, the Florida defenders were in perfect position to thwart them.

"Things completely turned around," Field said. "They shut us down like they knew every move we were going to make before we made it. For example, the information on the wristband outlined the four or five plays we used on short yardage. So it was a tremendous advantage for the defense to know what was coming."

The Gators shut out LSU in the second half and rallied to a 13–10 victory. Only after the game was over did Florida return the stolen wristband. A Gator coach gave it to an official, saying that one of his players "found" it on the field. The referee returned the wristband to Coach Dietzel.

"Even though they stopped us cold in the second half, I didn't suspect the Gators had access to our plays during the game," said Dietzel. "It was only afterward that I felt we'd been had.

"The Florida coaches didn't actually steal anything from us. They picked up something we lost and took advantage of it. Most people would have considered it good sportsmanship to return it when they found it."

Added Field, with sarcasm dripping from his voice, "It was nice of the Florida people to return the wristband after the game. They could have sold it to our next opponent."

CHICK MEEHAN

Coach ■ Syracuse Orangemen ■ Oct. 8, 1921

Syracuse coach Chick Meehan came up with a sneaky scheme that literally deflated the Maryland offense. He let just enough air out of the game ball to neutralize the Terrapins' star kicker.

Meehan was still smarting over a 10–7 upset to Maryland the year before. What really stuck in his craw was that halfback Ed "Untz" Brewer—the Terrapins' "Mr. Everything"—had almost single-handedly beaten his favored Orangemen.

Throughout that game, Brewer kept Syracuse pinned deep in its own territory with his booming punts—including a 60-yarder and a 72-yarder. He also ran for a touchdown and booted the winning field goal from 36 yards out.

Meehan plotted his revenge. Finally, he hit upon a devilish plan to frustrate Brewer and thwart his amazing kicking abilities.

When the two teams met again in 1921, the shifty coach deflated every available football so that the Maryland punter couldn't boot his kicks very high or far. The underhanded ploy worked to perfection.

Brewer's iron leg looked as though it had turned to jelly. His once-soaring punts traveled no more than a feeble 25 yards and were so short that they consistently left Syracuse with excellent field position.

The Orangemen capitalized on almost every weak punt to score a touchdown. Maryland tried to fight back and moved into field-goal range three times. But the usually reliable Brewer had lost his kicking oomph and all of his field-goal attempts fell woefully short. Syracuse went on to avenge its loss of the year before by crushing the duped Terrapins 42–0.

"Brewer had the worst kicking day of his life," recalled Roy Simmons, who played in the game for the Orangemen and later coached them. "Even the Maryland coach couldn't figure it out. He said, 'Geez, I've never seen Brewer kick like that.' Of course, they didn't know what Meehan had done to the balls."

Although Meehan got away with the chicanery, he became the victim of his own trickery two years later in 1923. He wanted to have more outside running room for his speedy halfback Chet Bowman (who would go on to win a silver medal in the 100-meter dash in the 1924 Olympics).

"We widened the field a few yards without anyone realizing it so we could take advantage of Bowman's speed on the outside," said Simmons. "But that cost us in the Colgate game." The Red Raiders completed a long bomb that the receiver caught just inside the sidelines for the winning touchdown. Said Simmons, "It would have been out of bounds had we not widened the field."

SILENT MIGHT

Gallaudet, the famed college for the hearing-impaired, took on a cocky bunch of collegiate all-stars in a 1912 game.

The all-stars, known as the Norfolk Blues, were so arrogant they didn't huddle up or call signals. Instead, they talked openly about what play to run because they figured Gallaudet's deaf players couldn't hear them.

But the Norfolk Blues forgot one thing. The Gallaudet players were expert lip readers! Gallaudet whipped Norfolk 20–0.

WILD BILL KELLY

Quarterback-Punter ■ Montana Grizzlies ■ Oct. 11, 1924

Wild Bill Kelly was a first-team All-America con artist.

The Montana Grizzlies star proved he could have sold screen doors for submarines when he suckered the Idaho coach into a timely 15-yard penalty.

Kelly was one of the greatest players in Montana history. On this day in 1924, he tried to spur his team to victory with a 70-yard punt return for a touchdown. But his heroics couldn't save the Grizzlies from what turned out to be a 41–13 drubbing by the Idaho Vandals. Facing a hopeless cause late in the game, Kelly resorted to the first rule of the con job: If you can't beat 'em, cheat 'em!

The Grizzlies were pushed back to their own goal line and forced to punt on fourth and 20. Standing deep in his own end zone with no room to maneuver, Kelly feared a blocked punt and further humiliation. So he set his sting operation in motion.

Wild Bill suddenly turned and walked toward the Idaho bench, waving his arms and calling for Vandals coach Robert Lee "Matty"

UNIVERSITY OF MONTANA SPORTS INFORMATION

Mathews. Puzzled by the punter's actions, Mathews walked out onto the field to meet Kelly. An equally bewildered referee, George Varnell, blew his whistle to stop the clock and joined the pair.

Kelly turned to the official and asked, "Mr. Varnell, you're acquainted with Mr. Mathews, the Idaho coach, aren't you?"

"Yes, of course," replied the perplexed ref.

"Then," continued Kelly slyly, "you must know that as the coach of the team, he's not supposed to be out on the playing field, is he?"

The referee was left with even less room to maneuver than Kelly. He tossed the flag and marked off the 15-yard penalty that gave Wild Bill room to punt his team out of a hole.

Successfully snookered, Mathews could only slink back to the sideline shaking his head in embarrassment.

BOYD CHAMBERS

Coach ■ Marshall Thundering Herd ■ Nov. 6, 1915

Marshall University coach Boyd Chambers devised a trick pass that stretched the rules of fair play literally to new heights.

Following Chambers' instructions, a receiver stood on the shoulders of a teammate in the end zone and caught a touchdown pass while the defenders below could do nothing but watch in frustration. It was, said the local newspaper with more than a little exaggeration, a pass play "that shocked the world."

Unfortunately for Marshall, the towering play was the Thundering Herd's only score during an otherwise embarrassing 92–6 thrashing by the West Virginia Mountaineers.

Before the end of the first half, it was clear that the Herd wouldn't be thundering over anyone as West Virginia raced to a 38–0 lead with ridiculous ease. Since the game was already lost, Chambers figured now was as good a time as any to unveil his latest scheme.

With the ball on the West Virginia 3-yard line, Marshall quarterback Brad Workman took the snap and scrambled in the backfield while eligible tackle Blondie Taylor and right end Dayton Carter dashed into the end zone. There, Taylor bent over and the smaller Carter climbed onto his shoulders. Then both stood up.

As the Mountaineer defenders crowded around the base of the human tower, Workman lobbed a pass high over their heads. Carter caught the ball and then tumbled to the ground for a Marshall touchdown.

"The air was charged with laughter, bewilderment and cheers when the historic play was staged," said the *Huntington Herald-Dispatch*. "The stands roared. History had been made in the twinkling of an eye.

"The [extra point attempt] was not made and Marshall's total for the afternoon's work was six points, yet Boyd Chambers, who up to the time had gained the title of 'Old Fox,' will be known forever as 'King of the Foxes.'

"It was a shame that an assist column is not afforded in football. If it were, [Blondie] Taylor would be given one big mark."

After the game, West Virginia coach Charles Metzger argued that the touchdown shouldn't have counted because the receiver technically was not on the field when he caught the pass. But referee John Butler countered that a receiver who leaps in the air to catch a pass is not on the field either, yet his reception counts. And since there was no specific rule against Chambers' human tower, he let the play stand. "You can rest assured," Butler told Metzger, "that the rules committee will legislate against the play by next season."

The ref was right. The rulemakers declared the play illegal the following year and chopped Chambers' human tower down to size.

BALDY ZABEL

Referee ■ Nov. 24, 1919

Captain Curly Lambeau and his Green Bay Packers were mugged by referee Baldy Zabel in one of the most blatant daylight robberies in pro football history.

The Packers were set up for the ambush when they agreed to meet a team called the Beloit Professionals (nicknamed the Fairies) on Beloit's home turf for the so-called 1919 "state championship of Wisconsin."

Beloit won 6–0 in a tainted victory that would have made Jesse James beam with pride. Zabel was from Beloit and to make sure his side won, the biased ref:

- Penalized the Packers each time they scored, disallowing the touchdowns
- Gave the Pros another five seconds to score the only touch-

down of the game—after time had already expired in the first half

• Let Beloit boosters swarm onto the field to stymie the Packers' passing attack

• Looked the other way when a fan tripped a Green Bay runner on his way to a certain touchdown.

On their first possession of the game, the previously undefeated Packers discovered that they had entered a den of thieves. Just as the Pack was about to score from the 5-yard line, Zabel personally made sure they wouldn't. On a touchdown run, the ref blew his whistle and penalized the Packers 15 yards for holding even though there wasn't any. That crippled the Green Bay drive. The Pros eventually took over on downs and both teams waged a defensive battle.

With time running out in the first half, the Pros had a first and goal on Green Bay's 5-yard line. But the Packers held on four straight plays and were ready to take over on downs when Zabel again tipped the balance in favor of the home team. He called Green Bay for being off sides on the fourth-down play. The penalty moved the ball to the 1-yard line (according to the rules at the time) and gave Beloit four more shots at a touchdown.

Just then, the timekeeper fired the gun, ending the first half. But Zabel decided the timekeeper was all wet and declared there were still five seconds left on the clock. Zabel ignored the Packers' protests and granted the Pros time for one more play. Beloit took full advantage of Zabel's gift and scored a touchdown on the final play of the extra-long half. The Pros went to the locker room with a 6–0 lead.

Zabel resumed his pillaging of the Pack in the second half. At one point, Lambeau threatened to pull his team off the field when Zabel tried to enforce a penalty against Green Bay by citing an obsolete rule from an out-of-date rule book.

But Zabel saved his larcenous best for last.

Despite the lopsided odds, Green Bay drove to the 5-yard line in the fourth quarter. Lambeau took the ball on third down, cut off tackle, and sliced cleanly into the end zone for the tying score.

But the cheating ref ruled that Lambeau's forward motion was stopped on the 2-yard line and that the touchdown didn't count. The Packers erupted like a spewing volcano and the game threatened to dissolve into a full-scale riot.

Finally, when it became obvious that Green Bay had no chance of winning the argument, Lambeau called the Packers back into the huddle. He warned them that Zabel would be looking for any excuse to prevent a Green Bay score and cautioned his teammates against holding or jumping offsides on their next play.

Again, the Green Bay line opened a big hole and Lambeau plunged into the end zone with room to spare. But incredibly, Zabel blew his whistle and signaled that the touchdown was no good! He called an offsides infraction against the Pack and penalized them five yards. Green Bay failed to score on the next play and Beloit took over on downs.

Meanwhile, Beloit fans had surrounded the field. During the last ten minutes of the game, Zabel allowed them to swarm onto the gridiron whenever the Packers had the ball. The fans harassed Green Bay receivers in a mob scene that made it impossible for Lambeau to pass.

When the Packers objected, Zabel merely shrugged and turned his back. On Green Bay's final possession late in the fourth quarter, a runner broke free and was streaking down the sideline for an apparent touchdown. But a Beloit fan stuck out his foot and tripped the ball carrier. The Packers protested, but Zabel said he didn't see the dastardly deed.

That was Green Bay's last opportunity to score and the game ended with Beloit—thanks to Baldy Zabel—ahead 6–0.

Green Bay officials and fans were outraged over Baldy's bald-faced heist.

"Robbery expresses the sentiment of everyone from Green Bay," said Packers coach W. J. Ryan. "The boys displayed a wonderful fighting ability, but it was simply a case of too much Zabel. One of the players put it well when he said, 'Beloit had the game won before we even stepped on the field.'"

Green Bay team official C. N. Murphy called the game "the most deliberate steal I have ever seen. It was a cut-and-dried deal to give Green Bay the worst of it, and they [Beloit] succeeded 100 percent."

The Packers argued in vain for a chance to even the score. They offered a $5,000 winner-take-all bet if Beloit would meet them on a neutral field with neutral referees. When the offer was rejected, the Pack even volunteered to go back to Beloit for a rematch. The Pros agreed, but later backed out.

"They knew they couldn't win without cheating," said a disgusted Green Bay fan. "The game was nothing short of highway robbery. The only things lacking were the masks and guns."

There are some things the world could do just fine without. War . . . famine . . . pestilence . . . team mascots. Who needs them? Fans go to the stadium to watch the game, not some animal who flunked Housebreaking 101 or some waddling, squawk-ing, Sesame Street—type mutant. For "The Silliest Performances by Mascots," The Football Hall of SHAME inducts the follow-ing:

AUBURN WAR EAGLE

Mascot ▪ Auburn Tigers ▪ Oct. 30, 1976

Wes Chandler scored the winning touchdown and got the bird from Auburn—literally!

Seconds after Chandler dashed across the goal line to give the University of Florida a dramatic come-from-behind victory, Auburn's mascot, the War Eagle, swooped from its perch and attacked the standout wide receiver.

And while Chandler frantically beat off the bird, the referee flagged the fowl and assessed a 15-yard penalty against Auburn for "illegal participation by the mascot."

"Nobody from Auburn could stop Chandler," commented Flor-ida's sports information director John Humenik. "Even the bird tried and failed."

Normally, the War Eagle remained placidly on its perch during Auburn games, acting more like a turkey on a Valium diet than a daring bird of prey. But against Florida in Gainsville, the eagle grew increasingly agitated as Chandler tore through the Auburn secondary.

In the second quarter, Chandler teamed up with quarterback Jimmy Fisher on a 44-yard touchdown pass that kept alive the Gators' hopes of winning their sixth straight of the year.

But with time running out in the fourth quarter, Florida still trailed the Tigers 19–17 when Chandler took an Auburn punt and ran it back for what appeared to be the go-ahead score. But a clip brought the ball back and the Gators started again from their own 20-yard line.

Recalled Chandler, "On the very next play, I caught a slant-in pass over the middle, reversed my field three or four times, and went 80 yards through the entire Auburn secondary for a touchdown. This one counted and we went ahead.

"The last Auburn defender who had a shot at me dove and missed. When I looked back, he was face down on the ground, pounding his fists on the turf in frustration. Just about that time, I heard a loud squawk and the bird bit me. Scared the hell out of me, because I didn't know what it was. It started going peck-peck-peck all over me. It probably would have hurt if I didn't have the pads on.

"Here were all those Auburn defenders who never touched me and the mascot was their last chance. It was like it was saying, 'OK. If you guys can't get him, then I will!' " Chandler said.

Officials marked off the 15-yard penalty against Auburn on the ensuing kickoff. The attack of the War Eagle failed to inspire the Tigers. They lost 24–19.

BIG AL THE ELEPHANT

Mascot ■ Alabama Crimson Tide

BABY POUNCER THE TIGER

Mascot ■ Memphis State Tigers
Sept. 16, 1989

Big Al and Baby Pouncer almost made the endangered mascots list when they were flagged for unsportsmanlike conduct and drew 15-yard penalties against their teams.

It was the only time in college football history that both teams' mascots were penalized for their on-field antics at the same time.

Southeastern Conference referee Rom Gilbert assessed the off-setting penalties at the start of the 1989 Alabama–Memphis State game in Birmingham.

"Oklahoma was penalized for letting its Sooner Schooner go on the field during the Orange Bowl one year," recalled Gilbert. "But as far as I know, this was the first time both mascots were penalized. They had been warned. They knew they were making a nuisance of themselves and were out of line."

Gilbert said the trouble started during the coin toss when no one but team members and officials are allowed on the field. Alabama's mascot, Big Al, who wore an elephant head complete with a trunk and floppy ears, was prancing on the gridiron. Field Judge Joe De-Lany warned Big Al that he was encroaching and had better hustle off to the sidelines fast.

"Joe asked Big Al to leave one time and the elephant talked back," recalled Gilbert. "When we asked him to leave the second time, he wised off again, so Joe threw the flag on him."

Debbie Brown, Alabama's cheerleader coach, saw it the other way around—that the coin toss was intruding while the mascots were on the field cavorting.

"There is a rule about not being on the field during the coin toss, but they don't enforce it all the time," she complained. "I don't see why they had to pick on Big Al. Our whole 300-piece band was on the field, too.

"The official told Coach [Bill] Curry that the mascots were misbehaving, which made him angry, and that upset me. This was Big Al. He wouldn't have done anything wrong.

"Some mascots, when you get on them, act belligerent and put up their fists like they want to fight back. Big Al doesn't do that. He's a cuddly, lovable-type character. But the official grabbed Big Al's trunk and tried to yank the poor guy's head off. I thought that was pretty harsh."

Right after Big Al drew the flag, Gilbert saw Baby Pouncer, Memphis State's mascot, dressed up like a tiger, running around on the field. So a second yellow flag came out.

"He [the Tiger] really was sort of a victim of circumstances," Gilbert admitted. "But he knew he wasn't supposed to be out there, so we had to flag him, too."

Big Al and Baby Pouncer were called on the carpet by coaches Bill Curry of Alabama and Chuck Stobart of Memphis State and warned that any more such mischief would lead to open season on mascots.

Said Memphis State's sports information director Bob Winn: "We passed the word to the Tiger to keep his butt off the field during the coin toss. Or else."

SEBASTIAN THE IBIS

Mascot ■ University of Miami Hurricanes ■ Sept. 28, 1989

University of Miami mascot Sebastian the Ibis tried to douse a flaming Florida State tradition. But his antics nearly landed him in jail.

"All I wanted to do was dampen their school spirit a little," said Sebastian, whose alter ego is John Routh. "But as soon as I stepped on the field, I was hammered by the cops. They really ruffled my feathers."

The Ibis blew into Doak Campbell Stadium in Tallahassee along with the rest of the Miami Hurricanes to participate in their heated rivalry with the Seminoles. He came equipped with a fireman's hat, slicker, and fire extinguisher. Sebastian's target was the famous blazing spear of FSU mascot Chief Osceola.

Before the start of every FSU home game, a student dressed as Chief Osceola gallops out on a horse named Renegade to the center of the field and dramatically plants a flaming lance as a symbol of a Seminoles victory.

Equipped with his borrowed fireman's gear, Sebastian hid in the locker room until it was time for the ceremony to begin and then ran out onto the field just as Chief Osceola prepared to launch the spear.

But the Miami mascot didn't count on the local police, who weren't about to let some weird bird that looks like a deranged Donald Duck dampen their traditional ceremony.

"Four of them grabbed me and slammed me up against a fence," Sebastian said. "One of them twisted my wing behind my back, another had his elbow on my throat, and one was trying to pull my head off [see photo].

"I thought it was kind of funny that the police, who were supposed to be in charge of crowd control, picked on the poor mascot instead. It wasn't exactly police brutality, but it sure was Ibis brutality."

During the struggle, the fire extinguisher accidentally sprayed the cops. "That really upset them," Sebastian said. "One of them pulled out his handcuffs and said he was going to throw me in jail. We argued back and forth, jaw to beak. The students around us were yelling to let me go."

Sebastian's fire extinguisher was confiscated and he was pinned against the fence until the flaming spear ceremony ended. But for the rest of the game, two officers tailed the plucked bird wherever he went.

"I guess they wanted to make sure I didn't leave any droppings on the field," said Sebastian.

THOR

Mascot ■ Atlanta Falcons ■ Sept. 11, 1966

The Atlanta Falcons mascot—a trained falcon named Thor—flew the coop before the team had even taken its first snap!

The menacing bird of prey had been selected as the majestic symbol of the NFL's latest expansion team in 1966. The Falcons' owners wanted a mascot that projected an image of grace, power, speed, and daring. What they hatched instead was a dodo bird.

Thor made his debut at the team's very first game before a packed house in Atlanta Stadium that included the governor, the mayor, the commissioner of the NFL, and other dignitaries. The inaugural pageantry centered around the exciting introduction of the team members as well as Thor, who had been painstakingly trained to participate in the ceremonies.

The event was carefully choreographed. Just as the team charged onto the field, Thor was to be released by his trainers, dramatically circle over the stadium three times in graceful, swooping dives, and then return to his perch while the crowd of 54,000 fans cheered their new heroes.

That was the Falcons' plan. Thor had his own agenda.

Right on cue, the door leading from the locker room to the field burst open and the Atlanta Falcons—decked out in their spanking new red, white, and black uniforms—dashed onto the field for their first-ever game.

Thor then made his grand entrance. He winged his way skyward.

He then took one turn around the field, soared high over the stadium—and disappeared!

"I was the first one out on the field," recalled Falcons receiver Alex Hawkins. "I got there just in time to wave bye-bye to the birdie.

"That was a pretty embarrassing way to kick off a whole franchise. Falcons may be a vanishing breed, but this was ridiculous."

Perhaps the bird had a premonition that something bad would happen to the team and he didn't want to stick around to watch. If so, he was right. The Los Angeles Rams clipped the Falcons' wings 19–14.

Despite the setback—losing Thor, not the game—the front office tried to repeat the falcon fly-by with Thor II, Thor III, and Thor IV. But just like the original Thor, they all flew away and never returned. Finally, when it got too expensive to keep freeing more Thors, the Falcons gave up the idea and concentrated on losing football games instead of losing birds.

BOWS-O

Mascot ■ University of Hawaii Rainbows ■ 1989

In the shortest reign in the history of college mascots, the University of Hawaii's Bows-O was booed, benched, and banished three days after making its debut.

The Associated Students of the University of Hawaii (ASUH), the student governing body, shelled out $1,600 for what it hoped would be a new mascot that would inspire respect, reverence, and even fear in opponents.

What the ASUH got for its bucks looked like a wimpy reject from a Roger Rabbit movie. The pink, marshmallow-headed, gap-toothed creature had a goofy grin, Barney Rubble eyes, and wore a squashed-down, cartoon version of a football helmet.

The ridiculous-looking mascot made its debut at Aloha Stadium during the 1989 homecoming game—and instantly bombed. Little kids accosted Bows-O before it ever reached the field and delivered well-placed kicks and punches to its ugly anatomy. The crowd in the stands greeted its first appearance with a shower of debris, catcalls, and insults.

Within minutes of its introduction, Bows-O had been hooted into oblivion. Three days later, the ASUH called an emergency session and voted Bows-O out of business.

"Actually, Bows-O wasn't its official name," said Mark Takai, president of the ASUH. "We sponsored a contest to give it a name that coincided with the university's nickname, the Rainbows. But before we found a winner, everybody was calling it Bows-O and the name stuck, much to our embarrassment."

Bows-O actually followed in the footsteps of other failed UH mascots. A Hawaiian warrior mascot had been canned because the dominant male figure offended female students. Later, a menehune, an island deity, was tried and rejected since native Hawaiians considered its use as a mascot both an ethnic and a religious insult.

"Since we couldn't use either the menehune or the warrior, the senate voted for a neutral, comic mascot—like the characters at Disneyland or the San Diego Chicken," said Takai. "But Bows-O apparently offended everybody!"

BOOING THE BOOSTERS

Fans come to the stadium to watch a game and engage in one of America's favorite pastimes—booing. At the whistle-happy ref, the fumble-fingered runner, the color-blind passer. But sometimes the real boos shouldn't be directed toward the playing field, but right up in the stands where fans have displayed some of the rowdiest conduct this side of a riot zone. For "The Most Outlandish Behavior of Fans," The Football Hall of SHAME inducts the following:

THE DAWG POUND

Cleveland Municipal Stadium ■ Oct. 1, 1989

The rabid fans in Cleveland's "Dawg Pound" flunked obedience school.

Because of their abusive behavior, the Browns gained an unfair advantage and a tainted victory over the visiting Denver Broncos.

When the Broncos were bombarded with a barrage of batteries, dog biscuits, and eggs launched from the Dawg Pound, referee Tom Dooley moved the game to the other end of the field. The bizarre move put Denver out of reach of the barking bleacher hounds. But it also meant that the Browns had a strong wind at their backs for most of the second half.

As a result, Cleveland kicker Matt Bahr booted two field goals, including a 48-yarder in the fourth quarter that, thanks to the wind, "cleared the crossbar by one or two coats of paint," Bahr admitted. The wind-assisted field goal gave the Browns a 16–13 victory.

The Dawg Pound is at the end of Cleveland Stadium where the seats are only a few feet away from the end zone. It got its name in 1984 when cornerback Hanford Dixon labeled the Browns' defensive unit "the Dawg Defense." He started barking at opponents and exhorted the fans in the end zone seats to do likewise. Those fans quickly became known as the Dawgs and showed up wearing outlandish canine costumes. They barked and howled like a pack of street dogs in heat. Whenever opposing teams came within range, the wild Dawgs littered the end zone with hard dog biscuits and imitation doggie droppings.

But their muttish behavior really turned wild when the Broncos came to town.

Early in the fourth quarter, with Denver starting a drive from its own 4-yard line, the Dawg Pound erupted. Biscuits, batteries, eggs, and even rocks were lobbed at the Broncos. Quarterback John Elway, who had complained of a similar dog-biscuit deluge during the 1986 AFC title game in Cleveland, said of the 1989 game: "Three of our guys got hit with eggs. Keith Bishop got one right in the face, and everybody was getting hit with dog bones. We were really getting pelted."

Referee Dooley urged the Dawgs to behave, but without success. "They threw a double-A battery that hit me on the head. I thought I had them calmed down, but then they threw a rock. Then another egg hit a Bronco, one landed in the middle of the Denver huddle, and someone else got hit with another double-A battery. That's when I stopped it and went to the other end of the field."

A few plays later, the Browns recovered a Denver fumble. With five seconds left, and the score tied at 13–13, Bahr had the wind at his back as he booted the winning field goal.

This wasn't the first time Cleveland fans forced teams to switch ends of the field. In 1978, the Houston Oilers came under a barrage of snowballs, cans, and bottles from unruly fans, forcing officials to move the teams to the opposite end. That game also was decided by a last-minute field goal, only it was the Oilers who booted one through the uprights to beat the Browns.

Denver's defensive coordinator, Wade Phillips, was with the Oilers at the time. "They weren't the Dawgs back then," Phillips said. "We just called them idiots."

PAUL HORNUNG FAN

Los Angeles Coliseum ■ Dec. 8, 1957

A beautiful die-hard Paul Hornung fan barged down to the Green Bay Packers bench during a game and refused to leave until she had her picture taken with her hero.

The Golden Boy couldn't resist the pleadings of such a shapely young miss, so he had his photo taken with her—and wound up in a heap of trouble.

When Hornung, a handsome bachelor fresh out of Notre Dame, signed with the Packers in 1957, girls swooned over him. They waited at his training camp doorstep, causing Packers coach Lisle Blackbourn to holler at Hornung, "There won't be any girls in my camp!"

From then on, Blackbourn was on Hornung's case about the fun-loving rookie's late-night penchant for wine, women, and song. Somehow Hornung managed to avoid any major hassles with Blackbourn until near the end of the season, when the Packers were in Los Angeles to play the Rams.

A few nights before the game, Hornung, who was nursing an injured ankle and wasn't expected to play against the Rams, spent the whole night squiring a pretty Hollywood starlet. He didn't return to the team's hotel until 8 A.M.

"I was coming into the hotel in my suit and tie, and it was a dead giveaway," he recalled. "Blackbourn called me in. He warned me: 'One more escapade like that, and I'll fine you your salary even if you're not going to play.' "

During the game, which the Rams won 42–17, Hornung was all suited up and sitting on the bench, minding his own business. Early in the fourth quarter, he heard a female voice calling, "Paul! Paul!" He turned around and spotted a gorgeous brunette standing in the front row of the Los Angeles Coliseum stands. "I want to take a picture with you," she said.

"Wait until after the game," Hornung replied.

"No, right now," she insisted.

Hornung cast a wary eye down to the end of the bench at Blackbourn, hoping the coach hadn't noticed the girl. This was no time to fool around. "Shhh," Hornung nervously whispered to her. "We'll do it after the game."

Fullback Howie Ferguson, who was sitting next to Hornung, watched the scene unfold and told him, "She's beautiful."

"I don't care how beautiful she is," countered the Golden Boy, now somewhat frantic that he was about to wind up in hot water. "If Coach catches me, he'll fine me my salary. He told me he wanted no more shenanigans."

Moments later, Ferguson elbowed Hornung and said, "Guess what? She's walking over here."

The girl tapped Hornung on the shoulder, leaned over, and whispered in his ear, "I'm not leaving until I get a picture." Hornung wheeled around and to his stunned amazement saw that she wasn't kidding. She had a photographer in tow! Rather than debate the issue or have her cause a scene, Hornung jumped up and moved behind the bench.

While the Packers were trying to score their first touchdown of the day, Hornung reluctantly put his arm around the girl, forced a smile, and had his picture taken with her.

"Now get out of here," he told her. "Meet me at the locker room entrance after the game. I want to talk to you."

Hornung thought he had pulled it off without Blackbourn seeing anything. But just as the girl and the photographer headed from the bench to the stands, Blackbourn turned around and spotted them. He also saw Hornung pivot and sit down. Although he couldn't quite figure out what had happened, the coach knew that Hornung was up to no good.

The Packers had just scored, so Blackbourn came up with a devious punishment. "Hornung!" he shouted. "Go in there and kick off!"

Even though Hornung was injured, he hobbled out onto the field on his sore ankle. "I knew I couldn't kick off, but I figured I had to go out and try," he recalled. "So I kicked the ball about five yards—beautiful. It went poof, poof, poof, and [Rams 250-pound guard] Duane Putman came up and hit me and I did two somersaults. With my bad ankle, I couldn't get out of the way. I came off that field with tears in my eyes. He almost killed me.

"There is a sad epilogue to this story. I did see the girl after the game, and I did get her number. Then I lost the damn thing."

NEW YORK GIANTS FANS

December 1978

New York Giants fans, in open revolt over the revolting play of their favorite team, took some of the most outrageous steps ever seen in the NFL to get their angry message across.

In 1978 they organized committees to sue management for non-support and to rename the team the New York Gnomes. They hung owner Wellington Mara in effigy—during a game. They burned their season tickets in protest. And they even took to the sky to announce their displeasure far and wide.

The airborne complaint appeared above Giants Stadium in the third quarter of the game against the St. Louis Cardinals on December 10. Towed by a small plane, the banner proclaimed: "15 YRS. OF LOUSY FOOTBALL. WE'VE HAD ENOUGH."

And in the stands, the 52,000 fans (there were 24,000 disgusted no-shows) rose to their feet and took up the chant: "We've had enough! We've had enough!"

Before the game, an organized group of fed-up fans even plotted legal action against their woeful team. Members of the Giants Fans Committee planned to take the New York team to court, claiming consumer fraud. The fans argued that season ticket holders were forced to buy tickets for eight home games even though the Giants were invariably out of contention by midseason. The fans wanted the court to force the Giants to give season subscribers a refund on 14 days' notice. (Their case never made it on the docket.)

The previous Sunday, when the Giants lost to the Los Angeles Rams, more than 100 fuming fans, frustrated after years of dismal defeats, gathered outside the Stadium gate and built a bonfire with their season tickets. They were upset that the Giants hadn't made the playoffs since 1963. In the five years leading up to the 1978 fan revolt, the team was an embarrassing 5–9; 3–11; 5–9; 2–12; and 2–11–1.

Said one disgusted ticket burner as he watched his hopes for a winning season go up in smoke: "Mara should send out [quarterback] Joe Pisarcik to fall on the fire and end it."

He referred to what has come to be known in Giant lore simply as "The Fumble," one of the most boneheaded plays in NFL history. It became the focal point of fan anger and sparked the firestorm of protest.

The Giants were already mired in a losing streak before they met the Philadelphia Eagles on November 19. After leading Atlanta, New Orleans, and Washington, the Giants blew each game, along with what little respect the fans had left for the franchise.

Then came the Philly game. Right to the end there was hope that the Giants might win one and halt the humiliating skid. No such luck. With only 28 seconds to play, the Giants had the ball and the Eagles were out of timeouts. All quarterback Pisarcik had to do was fall on the ball to ensure victory. Instead, to the horror of the fans, he botched a handoff to fullback Larry Csonka. Eagle cornerback Herman Edwards scooped up the loose ball and dashed over the goal line for the winning touchdown.

A shocked crowd staggered homeward following the horrible defeat, many of them muttering voodoo curses against the wretched Giants.

Others decided things had gone far enough. All the years of frustration were summed up in that classic boner. Fan Ron Freiman, of Livingston, New Jersey, took out an advertisement in the papers urging season-ticket holders to cut up their ducats and send them to him to fuel the bonfire outside the gates at the next home game "in memory of great Giant teams of past years."

Another group calling itself the Committee Against Mara Insensitivity to Giant Fans ran its own ad, calling for a mass protest rally before the December 10 Cardinal game to show management they were "mad as hell and not going to take it anymore."

The day the banner flew over the stadium, committee members passed out fliers to arriving fans proclaiming, "If you feel we Giant Fans have suffered long enough, pass this along the aisle to other Die Hard Giant Fans and join in a unison chant of 'We've Had Enough.' We have been the most supportive, loyal fans in the world. Maybe if we raise our voices, our message will reach management. We cannot wait another 15 years for a championship!"

The protest may have done some good. The Giants beat St. Louis that day. Sort of. But they had a lot of help from the Cardinals, who fumbled four times and dropped eight passes.

After that, things got back to their normal losing ways. The Giants dropped the last game of the season to finish with a 6–10 record.

MICHIGAN WOLVERINE FANS
CENTRAL MICHIGAN CHIPPEWAS FANS

1989

Fans in Michigan discovered a sticky way to torment their opponents, their own teams, and themselves—by throwing marshmallows!

Thousands of the puffy, gooey sweets littered the fields and made a mess of the stands during several early-season games at Michigan and Central Michigan.

The bizarre trend ended as quickly as it began in 1989 after officials at both universities announced that the next marshmallow chucker would get chucked right out on his ear.

The first marshmallow sailed through the air during Michigan's home game against Maryland on September 30. As usual, the Ann Arbor stadium was packed. And just as predictably, the game was a blowout.

A student who had brought a bag of marshmallows to snack on began tossing the treats at his friends to fend off the boredom. They threw the marshmallows back and an instant fad was born.

By the next home game, some entrepreneurs had set up stands outside the stadium gates and were peddling marshmallows at vastly inflated prices.

"For a couple of games, people were hauling in bags and bags of marshmallows until it just got insane," said Rick Eisen, the *Michigan Daily* sports editor. "The student section was literally covered with marshmallows. They got stuck in your hair and smeared all over your clothes. There were thousands of them!

"Against Wisconsin, hardly anybody was watching the game, which really wasn't worth watching anyway. They were too busy either throwing or ducking marshmallows."

The dimwitted craze ceased to be funny when fans mashed a handful of marshmallows into one big mess and soaked them in water until the softball-sized lumps were hard as rocks.

"Some alumni got hit and those are the folks who pay the bills," recalled Eisen. "There were a lot of complaints and that was the end of the marshmallows." School authorities announced that henceforth marshmallows would be banned.

Meanwhile, the movement had spread to the Central Michigan campus in Mt. Pleasant. The first slight shower of marshmallows appeared when the Chippewas played Kent State on October 7. It quickly grew to blizzard proportions. During the Youngstown State and Eastern Michigan games, it got so bad that police action was required to quell the marshmallow marauders.

After parents and alumni complained about the bombardment, the school administration took steps to squash the marshmallows. Students caught throwing the sugary treats were thrown out of the stadium.

"People were smuggling in bags of marshmallows," said Fred Stabley, Central Michigan's sports information director. "They threw them onto the field where they were stepped on and ground into the artificial surface. The weather was still warm enough so the marshmallows melted all over the place. It was a real sticky mess to clean up.

"It was one of those weird fads that's hard to explain. During basketball season, our fans throw rolls of toilet paper on the court when we score our first goal. I guess they just switched their allegiance from basketball and toilet paper to football and marshmallows."

CRAZY LEGS HIRSCH FANS

Los Angeles Coliseum ■ Dec. 12, 1954

Believing their hero had played his last game in the NFL, hundreds of youths stormed the field and stripped Los Angeles Rams star Crazy Legs Hirsch of everything he wore.

When the frenzy subsided, all the shorn Ram had left were his shorts and the tape on his ankles.

At halftime of the Rams' 35–27 victory over the Green Bay Packers, the retiring Hirsch was honored by the team for his outstanding career as a sticky-fingered, record-setting receiver. During the ceremonies, he was presented with a new Oldsmobile.

Later, when the final gun sounded, a swarm of about 500 young fans engulfed Crazy Legs in front of the Los Angeles bench in a wild search for a souvenir.

"After each game, I always tossed my chin strap into the crowd," recalled the Hall of Famer. "But this time, I saw right away that they

were after more because everyone, including me, thought that it was my last game.

"The kids came running onto the field and started tearing at my jersey. Somehow, they got me off my feet and I fell to the ground. I was afraid of getting trampled and I felt so helpless. They wouldn't let me up. One kid was pulling off my shoe, another one tearing at my jersey, and a third one trying to rip my belt. So I shouted, 'Hey! Back away and I'll take it all off. Just don't hurt me.'"

While sitting on the ground, Hirsch took off his jersey and threw it into the crowd. But the fans wanted more. They stripped the laces from his shoulder pads, then ripped off the shoulder pads and tore his T-shirt.

"Finally, I thought the hell with it, and I pulled off my shoes, my pants, my socks, and my stockings and threw them into the crowd," said Crazy Legs. "I was left with nothing on but my girdle hip pad [shorts with pads in them] and I wasn't about to take that off."

After leaving him all but bare, the fans let Hirsch flee unmolested to the locker room. "None of my teammates came to help me because they didn't realize what had happened," he said. "All I know is it was funny but frightening."

Ironically, it turned out that the game was not Crazy Legs' last hurrah. He changed his mind about retiring and played another three years.

But he had learned his lesson. When he finally did quit the game, he announced his retirement *after* the season was over.

THE PHANTOM POLICEMAN

Canton (Ohio) Park ■ Nov. 29, 1915

The scheming actions of one fan triggered one of the wildest rhubarbs in pro football history.

The brouhaha raged for so long that the game was called off with eight minutes left to play—and it took until the wee hours of the morning before an official statement announced the winner of the game.

The controversy erupted in the 1915 title game between the top two professional teams in football back then—Ohio's arch rivals, the Massillon Tigers and the Canton Bulldogs. Massillon, led by Notre Dame greats Gus Dorais and Knute Rockne, and Canton, which featured Jim Thorpe, had such a bloodthirsty rivalry that fans, players, and club officials bet heavily on the games.

The game at Canton's 8,000-seat park attracted such an overflow mob that spectators were allowed to stand in the end zones. So both teams agreed to a new ground rule that said any player crossing the goal line into the crowd must be in possession of the ball when he emerged from the crowd.

The game turned into a hard-fought, bruising defensive struggle, and midway through the final quarter Canton held a slim 6–0 lead, thanks to two field goals by Thorpe. But then Massillon engineered its only drive of the day and marched to the Canton 11-yard line.

From there, Dorais threw a pass to a player named Briggs, who then raced across the goal line and disappeared into the standing-room-only crowd. It looked like the game-tying touchdown. But suddenly, the ball popped out of the thick crowd and landed right in the hands of Canton tackle Charley Smith.

Referee Ed Connors, mindful of the ground rule made before the game, called the play a touchback. But Briggs protested. "I didn't fumble!" he declared. "That ball was kicked out of my hands by a policeman."

"How could you tell?" said a Canton player. "There are no policemen in uniform here."

"It was a policeman," Briggs insisted. "I saw the brass buttons on his coat."

Players and referees heatedly debated the play for 20 minutes until the spectators couldn't stand the tension any longer. They swarmed onto the gridiron by the thousands. The officials tried desperately to clear the field and resume play, but it was futile. So they called the game with eight minutes left to play.

But no one was sure of the game's outcome. Fans and players wanted a firm ruling on the play because both teams had a lot at stake. The unofficial 1915 championship was on the line. If the touchdown was allowed, then the game would end in a 6–6 tie, making Massillon the undisputed champion because it had already beaten Canton earlier in the season. If Connors' call of a touchback was allowed to stand, Canton would win 6–0 and thus share the title.

Massillon and its loyal supporters demanded that the referees settle the matter once and for all by making an official statement. The refs agreed—but on the condition that the statement be sealed and given to the manager of the Courtland Hotel where it would be read at 30 minutes after midnight. That way, the officials would have plenty of time to flee town and escape the wrath of one of the teams and its rabid fans who were sure to explode over the ruling.

Throughout the evening, tension built to a feverish pitch as fans crammed into the hotel lobby. Finally, it was time to read the statement. The officials had declared the play was a touchback, saying it was proper under the ground rules. As a result, the Canton Bulldogs won 6–0 and tied the Massillon Tigers for the championship.

Not until 10 years later was the mystery of the Phantom Policeman solved. Bulldog manager Jack Cusack was riding a streetcar in Canton when he struck up a conversation with the conductor, who was clad in a brass-buttoned uniform. They began reminiscing about the infamous 1915 Canton-Massillon game. The conductor then told Cusack the truth about what really happened on that controversial play: "When Briggs plunged across the goal line into the end-zone crowd, he fell at my feet. So I promptly kicked the ball from his hands and it went right into the arms of Charley Smith."

"Why on earth did you do a thing like that?" Cusack asked.

"Well," the conductor said, "it was like this. I had thirty dollars bet on that game and, at my salary, I couldn't afford to lose that much money."

WHO ELSE BELONGS IN THE FOOTBALL HALL OF SHAME?

Do you have any nominations for The Football Hall of SHAME? Give us your picks for the most shameful, funniest, embarrassing, wackiest, boneheaded moments in gridiron history. Here's your opportunity to pay a lighthearted tribute to the game we all love.

Please describe your nominations in detail. Those nominations that are documented with the greatest number of facts—such as firsthand accounts, newspaper or magazine clippings, box scores or photos—have the best chance of being inducted into The Football Hall of SHAME. Feel free to send as many nominations as you wish. If you don't find an existing category listed in our Football Hall of SHAME books that fits your nomination, then make up your own category. All submitted material becomes the property of The Football Hall of SHAME and is nonreturnable. Mail your nominations to:

The Football Hall of SHAME
P.O. Box 31867
Palm Beach Gardens, FL 33420